BEAD SETTING DIAMONDS

With

Pavé Applications

ROBERT R. WOODING

Published by DRY RIDGE CO.

P.O. BOX 18814   ERLANGER, KENTUCKY 41018

Library of Congress Card Catalog No. 85-073051

ISBN 0-9613545-2-6

Printed in the United States of America

CONTENTS (cont.)

To those who support my time consuming projects:

My wife,
        Marilyn Jo
My children,
        Tammy Jo—Cindy Jo—Wendy Jo—Bobby Jo—Mary Jo

IMPETUS

My first book, *DIAMOND SETTING: The Professional Approach* was written to fulfill a need to promote the communication of ideas and procedures of the craft. Since then other diamond setting books have been published in the United States and more are in the process of being published. I am satisfied now that a line of communications is being established. In effect, a multitude of inquiries have been stimulated and questions are being answered. One primary topic of increasing interest is pavé setting. *BEAD SETTING DIAMONDS: With Pavé* Applications is a response to those inquiries.

COVERAGE

Bead setting diamonds is the exclusive subject of the text. It is a diversification of the diamond setting field that has evolved into a departmental specialty in jewelry production establishments. Since bead setting is the fundamental procedure of pavé setting, emphasis is given to the development and expansion of that procedure. The instruction is detailed and illustrative, and encourages the reader to pursue and innovate alternative measures to problematic segments. From the outset I have written each segment to benefit the apprentice as well as the experienced diamond setter. However, the instruction is advanced diamond setting, and therefore includes information not found in books intended for the beginner.

ORGANIZATION

The book is partitioned into four sequential and interdependent sections. Section I goes beyond the scope of describing tools. It discusses their purposes, uses, and maintenance. Also, heat treating, graver shaping and sharpening, and different methods to make a beading tool are included. Section II clearly describes each phase of the bead setting procedure and the sub-components. The layout segment is empirically illustrated as the diamond setter's blueprint. Also special emphasis is given to preparing a flat graver for bright cutting. Section III applies the bead setting procedure to a variety of situations beginning with fundamental bead settings. Then it expands to configurations that resemble fancy shapes. Section IV defines and illustrates pavé setting. Various shapes of clusters are presented to explain the procedure. By the conclusion of the final segment the reader, who has practiced and adhered to the order of segments step by step, will have indulged in a thoroughly applied program of pavé diamond setting.

FEATURES

A number of training aids designed to enrich the instruction are included in the book. Special topics are presented to divert from the academics. Many of these discuss and give solutions to problems that often occur in the real world of diamond setting. Also, alternate methods to perform various segments of the bead setting procedures are discussed. Line drawings are inserted where a detailed description is necessary to completely understand certain phases. To show each phase of the procedure being applied to actual practice, photographs are included along with the text. An index is given for a quick page reference or review of specific terms and segments. And, suggested books to read and a list of diamond setting schools are available for those interested in furthering their occupational education.

THANKS

There are many persons whose contributions to this work must be acknowledged. In the order of production sequence they are: The students of Dry Ridge Diamond Setting School whose eagerness to learn sparked the enthusiasm needed to present the information; David R. Brown for his patience and photography expertise; The employees of Ric Lohrs Quickprint for their reproductions of line drawings, manuscript copies, and promotional materials; Robert A. Wainscott who unselfishly contributed his skills to copy edit and type the final draft; Melissa for her typing performance and serenity to instill the calmness at the most critical of times; Those remarkable employees of Alpha Typesetting whose conscientious dedication to their craft organized the manuscript, line drawings, and photographs into book form; And, Robert D. Lewis and Pat Bolling for expediting the final stages of production.

CONTENTS

CONTENTS (cont.)

SECTION I

Tool Preparation and Maintenance

Introduction

Handicraft occupations, those involving manual skills, require an assortment of universal and specialized tools. Diamond setting is no exception. Conventional machine tools such as grinding machines and drilling machines are necessary as well as an assortment of hand tools. Some are adopted from other trades, but many are innovated and altered for diamond setting within the jewelry industry. Since the illustrations in this book are devoted entirely to the specialization of bead setting diamonds, the tools listed and described for use are only those applicable to that purpose.

Besides the recommended tool list discussed in this section, a diamond setter will eventually innovate and make other tools at the bench. Like all mechanical crafts there is always a better way of doing things. Also there are orphan tools to be devised that tool manufacturers cannot profitably mass produce. Although some of these might seldom be used, they are occasionally convenient to have.

Three primary considerations concerning tools are the purpose, quality, and maintenance. Some tools are versatile in that they may have multiple purposes. In all cases professional work requires the best available tools not only for quality work, but also for extended use. To keep each tool in good condition, it should be used properly and cared for. Neglecting or abusing tools shows up in the work to which they are applied. During the description of each tool, reference will be made to these three concerns. For that reason, and the inclusion of other noteworthy comments, a considerable amount of attention should be given to this section.

1

Tool List

BEADING TOOLS

Beading tools are short rods of metal about one eighth inch diameter and two inches long. They are tapered at one end to a concave tip. The tips of beading tools range in size to accommodate a variety of bead sizes. By inserting the shaft into a wood handle, or the handpiece of a flex-shaft machine, it can be controlled to round off burs of metal that secure bead set diamonds (see Shape The Beads, pg. 77). This is done by twisting or revolving the concave tip on each burr.

Carbon tool steel capable of being heat treated at the workbench is necessary in a beading tool because it will have to be reshaped periodically. A set of beading tools listed in tool catalogues as "domestic' are recommended. The set contains twelve sizes but that is irrelevant. It is the susceptibility of the metal to be heat treated that is most important. The tips of the

Fig. 1-1. Beading tools with handle.

4

tools do not last long before they need reshaping. At that time the tips can be easily reshaped on the beading tool plate to any size (see Making A Beading Tool, pg. 32).

Some diamond setters make their own beading tools from handles of needle files or similar metal. This is acceptable when the tool will be used with a wood handle. However, there are times when a beading tool will be used in a flex-shaft machine (see Shape The Beads, pg. 77). Here the shaft of an original beading tool is necessary because it can be revolved true in the handpiece.

BEADING TOOL PLATE

A beading tool plate for standard size beads is used to reshape the tips of beading tools. This is done by a die-struck technique using a hammer (see Making A Beading Tool, pg. 32). Various sizes of plates are available, none of which are particularly recommended over the others. Only a trustworthy brand name need be suggested. They are all hardened steel, but the price will vary according to the number of embossed beads. Dimensions of a common plate are about three-eighths inch by one inch by two inches. It contains thirty-two embossed beads; four beads for each of the eight sizes. The extra number of beads for each size allows for wear and tear and abuse.

Beading tools should be annealed before reshaping, otherwise the beads on the plate will break prematurely. The plate is hardened and tempered for toughness but will not withstand the striking from a similarly hardened beading tool. Also a solid backing such as a bench block and sturdy workbench is necessary in order to adequately form the tip of the beading tool. If the beading tool is tapped against a plate that permits a vibration, the concave tip might not form properly.

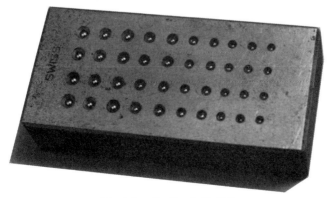

Fig. 1-2. Beading tool plate.

BEES WAX

Bees wax is a product that results from melting down honeybee combs after the honey is removed. It is available at many local drug stores. Some of its most popular uses after purification are as an ingredient in cosmetics and to weather-proof machinery. Diamond setters use pure bees wax as a lubricant for saw blades, for handling diamonds, and to lay out diamonds.

Pure bees wax is usually yellow or white and processed in cakes about one inch thick. When it is used for handling diamonds, only a small amount (about one square inch) is needed. It becomes brittle during storage and needs to be remelted to increase the pliability. Afterwards it can be formed by hand to any desired shape. Some diamond setters push a broken bur shaft or similar short rod of metal through it. By doing that it can be used as a versatile tool. The metal is used to push diamonds into bearings...turn the tool around and the tapered bees wax can be used to pick up diamonds simply by touching them.

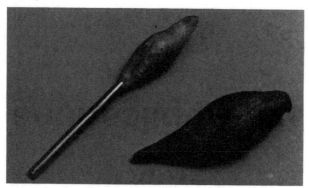

Fig. 1-3.   Bees wax formed for handling diamonds.

BENCH BLOCK

A bench block is a multi-purpose section of hardened steel. Generally, it should be stable, a reasonable size, and have a planed surface. An anvil will do if it is a small model that is not too large for a workbench top. Since it is used quite often, it should be close to the workbench. For that reason a smaller bench block about one inch by four inches is practical.

The primary purpose of a bench block during bead setting is to serve as a solid hammering surface for reshaping beading tools. Other uses are as a smooth and easy-to-clean surface to form diamond setters cement, and a fire-proof area to temporarily place heated tools and materials. Since the bench block is used most often in conjunction with the beading tool plate, the plate can ideally serve as a storage platform for that tool.

BENCH BRUSHES

Two types of brushes are used for diamond setting purposes. One is a hand brush to sweep the fell tray and to keep the workbench clean. The other is a common toothbrush used to remove filings and other debris from mountings during diamond setting procedures. Neither brush requires strict specifications just so they do the job.

Keeping the workbench clear of dust and other forms of debris is important for working conditions, and saves time when a diamond is lost. Busy diamond setters frequently maintain a cluttered workbench but suffer in the long run when a diamond is dropped. At that time the fell tray and possibly the workbench top has to be swept with the hand brush to search through the rubble for the lost diamond. Also, diamond setting is a detailed craft that requires precision work. Any obstruction on the miniature tools can have an adverse effect on the craftsmanship.

Too often a novice diamond setter becomes involved in the work and neglects to keep the mounting clean. This is especially important when bead setting because dirt, filings, and other debris cling to the coolant fluids and bees wax in the bearings. These materials must be removed in order to properly seat the diamonds. The smaller toothbrush is used for this purpose.

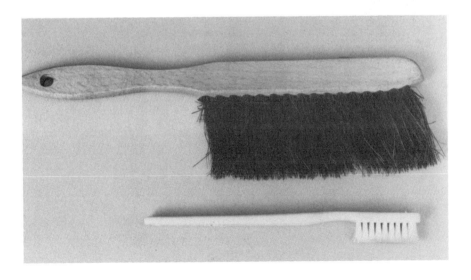

Fig. 1-4.   Bench Brushes.

BURS

Burs are small cutting tools of various shapes and sizes with a $\frac{3}{32}$ inch diameter shaft (some brands have slightly larger shafts). The slender shaft allows them to be inserted into the handpiece of the flex-shaft machine. They are used to excavate metal after drilling, to shape metal, and to cut bearings for diamonds. Diamond setters eventually develop their own style of bur use and choose a particular selection of burs to suit their needs.

Bead setting applications in this book illustrate the use of bud burs, high speed setting burs, and hart burs. These are recommended, but there is no intention to confine anyone to them. Many diamond setters perform excellently with other types of burs. Diamond setters should not be limited to any particular selection of burs because diamond setting procedures vary according to individual preference.

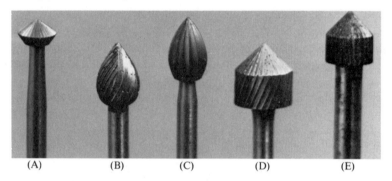

(A)   (B)   (C)   (D)   (E)

Fig. 1-5. (A) Hart bur, (B) high speed bud bur, (C) tungsten steel bud bur, (D) high speed seting bur, (E) stone setting bur.

TAPER BORING BURS

Bud burs are used, when bead setting, to remove excess metal from holes prior to cutting bearings. The holes should be taper bored to the approximate size of the diamonds being set. Taper boring prior to cutting the bearings allows setting burs to cut more accurately by eliminating the stress of excessive cutting. They also reduce wear and tear of the bearing cutting burs. Bud burs are available in either high speed or tungsten vanadium steel. The high speed tool steel is more expensive but will last longer. Either type is acceptable.

BEARING CUTTING BURS

Setting burs are used to cut bearings during bead setting procedures. High speed setting burs are recommended for quality. The expense is offset by the durability of the metal. Stone setting burs are not to be disregarded because they are useful but not so much for bead setting purposes. Different sizes of setting burs allow for a bearing to be cut that conforms to the shape of a round cut diamond. The upper section of the bur provides a straight bore in the metal while the bottom of the bur cuts a bearing to seat the pavilion of the diamond.

UNDERCUTTING BURS

Hart burs are primarily used to undercut metal. Undercutting is necessary in some situations when pavé setting diamonds close together. Often the design of the jewelry requires a hart bur to undercut a bead that is securing two diamonds (see Secure The Diamond, pg. 72). Also hart burs are occasionally used as setting burs, or when the exact size setting bur needed is not available. In that case the hart bur is used only after the largest available size of bearing cutting bur is used to precut the bearing.

COOLANTS

Coolants are used for metal cutting efficiency and preventing premature wear of tools. The coolant reduces friction, thus keeping the tools and mounting cool, and washing away chips and shavings from newly cut metal. The most effective types for high speed tool steel are natural petroleum oil (mineral oil), animal oil (lard oil), and sulfurized oil. Sulfurized oil is mineral oil or lard oil that has sulfur added. Other coolants commonly used by diamond setters are synthetic wintergreen oil, bees wax, and water. Each of these, except water, will leave a residue that should be removed before setting diamonds.

Some common applications of coolants are for drilling, taper boring, bearing cutting, and graver shaping and sharpening. Specifically: when cutting metal, the drill or bur should periodically be dipped into a tin pill box containing cutting fluid. This will reduce friction and have related benefits: saw blades, and sometimes drills and burs, are lubricated with bees wax; coolants are applied to oil stones for graver sharpening, and ground metal will float on the fluid, thereby leaving the grain open for efficient sharpening; and water is used to keep gravers cool when shaping them on a grinding machine.

DIAMOND SETTERS CEMENT

Diamond setters cement is used as a fixture to secure articles of jewelry that cannot be grasped by a ring clamp, particularly earrings, pendants, and bracelets. When heated it becomes soft and pliable allowing the jewelry to sink into it. After the cement cools, by dipping into water if preferred, diamonds can be set into the mounting. It is brittle but much tougher than shellac.

The cement fixture is called a cement stick. It is made at the bench by cutting about five or six inches of wood from a broom handle or similar wood dowel. A small portion of the cement is melted over a flame onto either or both ends of the stick. Molten cement will adhere to the wood but also drip until it is cooled. Heat the cement over the bench block to catch the excess. Occasionally dab the stick onto the cement that drips on the plate to pick up the loose drippings.

Fig. 1-6.   Diamond setters cement.

Fig. 1-7.   Cement stick.

DIVIDERS

Dividers are used to determine how many diamonds can be set into a particular mounting, spacing of diamonds, and other precise layout judgments. They can be used in the same manner as a compass or as a measuring device. The steel points act as scribers to engrave the softer precious metals. Circles, arcs, and other border notations can be engraved on the metal. Usually trial and error is applied, but exact measurements can be transferred directly from the mounting and/or diamond.

When dividers are used as a compass, an indentation is first picked into the metal by a round graver, or center punch, at the center point where a diamond is to be set. The indentation serves to fix one point of the dividers while the other point is adjusted to the radius of the diamond. Then a circle can be engraved that is the diameter of the diamond being set there. The engraved circle becomes a border to ensure that all drilling, taper boring, and bearing cutting are done within a specified area. In this manner a series, or cluster, of diamonds can be layed out with reasonable accuracy.

Dividers are also used to engrave a consistant border near the edge of a metal plate where diamonds are to be set. For instance, a row of diamonds can be set into a straight path, or into a uniform curve, with each diamond at an equal distance from the edge. To do this the dividers are adjusted to the preferred distance that the girdles of the diamonds are to be from the edge of the plate. Then, with one point sliding along the outside edge of the plate, the other point is pressed on the plate to engrave the border.

Fig. 1-8. Dividers.

DRILLS

Twist drills are a necessity for bead setting diamonds as a prerequisite to taper boring and bearing cutting. Diamond setters use the straight shank type made of either high speed steel or carbon steel (see Drill The Hole, pg. 53). High speed steel is recommended because the temper of carbon steel drills is easily lost under normal working conditions. The sizes commonly used range between about No. 50 to No. 80 of the wire gauge. No. 50 (.07 inch) is the larger, and No. 80 (.135 inch) is the smaller. All sizes within this range are not necessary to have on hand, but a selection of small, medium, and large will be useful.

EMERY PAPER

Emery paper is an abrasive faced paper used to remove file marks and abrasions on jewelry prior to polishing. It is wrapped around a thin flat stick and used in a manner similar to that of a hand file. The grit sizes used for diamond setting are 4/0, 3/0, 2/0, 0, 1, 2, and 3. No. 3, the most course, is used to remove deep abrasions, and No. 4/0, the finest, is used to polish the metal. A common combination to remove abrasions is to first use a No. 3 followed by a No. 4/0.

Fig. 1-9.   Emery paper—polishing paper.

EYE LOUPES

Eye loupes provide the necessary close viewing for detail inspections of mountings, diamonds, and bead work. Two types available for diamond setting are monocular and binocular. Monocular loupes are used for one eye and binocular loupes are used for both eyes simultaneously. Each is used at the discretion of the individual diamond setter.

Some monocular loupes are in the form of one or two lens mounted into a tubular structure. This is the universal black eye loupe. However, a single lens fixed into a wire frame that is clipped onto the side of an eye glass frame is more accessible. For bead setting purposes a high powered loupe having 7X to 10X power is necessary. These powerful lens should be used primarily for inspection only, rather than continuous viewing.

Binocular loupes are acceptible for continuous use when working. These loupes provide close viewing for both eyes simultaneously, thereby offering dimensional viewing. Two common types are those attached to a headband, and those that clip onto the eyeglass frames. A power that offers a working distance of about five to seven inches is ideal for bead setting.

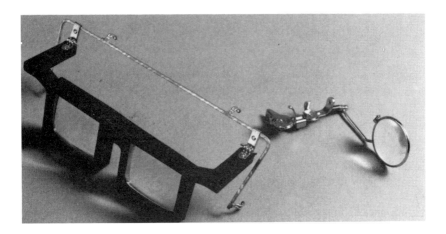

Fig. 1-10. Eye loupes (binocular and monocular).

FILES

Files are used to smooth and shape metal. For precision filing a Swiss pattern type is recommended. When bead setting diamonds it is often necessary to file the surface of plates even prior to beginning other work. Also, plate metal is trimmed after the diamonds are set to refine the intended design. The type of work being done will determine the shape, size, and coarseness of the file needed.

There are a variety of files that can be used for bead setting diamonds, but each individual will favor a selected few. Basically, a flat hand file is needed for smoothing larger flat surfaces, and a selection of smaller needle

types are used for trimming work. Common shapes of needle files are barrette, three square, square, round, half round, and oval. The coarseness of
cuts usually range between No. 00 to No. 6. The smaller number is more
coarse.

Fig. 1-11. Assorted needle files and flat hand file.

FLEX-SHAFT MACHINE

The flexible shaft machine powers the drills, burs, and other small tools.
A standard flex-shaft machine has $\frac{1}{10}$ h.p. Variable speeds up to 14,000
r.p.m. are obtainable and controlled by a foot rheostat. The handpiece may
either have a chuck that is adjustable to accept shafts up to $\frac{5}{16}$ inch ($\frac{1}{4}$ inch
in some late models), or a quick change-flip lever-chuck release. The quick
change models have a collet that will accept only one shaft size. That size
may vary but must be specified when purchased. All machines have a flexible shaft extending from the motor about forty inches allowing the handpiece to be maneuverable and accessible.

GRAVERS

Gravers are used for bead setting to engrave and displace metal. There
are several types, cutting shapes, and sizes of each shape. Basically only
three gravers are necessary to bead set diamonds. These are the straight type
of round, onglette, and flat. Variations of these and multiple sizes of each
usually account for a large inventory of gravers on a diamond setter's workbench. Gravers made of high speed steel are preferred because the metal has
the ability to retain sharpness.

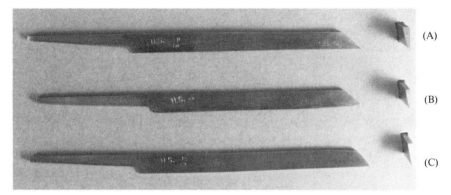

Fig. 1-12. High speed steel gravers (A) round, (B) onglette, (C) flat.

The primary purpose of *round* gravers is to pry burrs of metal onto diamonds to secure them (see Secure The Diamond, pg. 70). This is called "raising the beads" and is done after the diamonds are seated below the surface
of the metal. Various sizes of round gravers are available depending on the
size of beads wanted. Usually larger beads are raised on larger diamonds.

Onglette gravers are used to rough cut the metal away from diamonds
after the diamonds are secure (see Engrave Excess Metal), pg. 75). They
should be shaped to a narrow tip to avoid cutting off beads while removing
the metal behind them. Usually the graver is held at a slant in order to bevel
the metal. In this manner the cutting is done with one side of the cutting
edge.

Flat gravers are polished at the tip for bright cutting metal that sur-
rounds the diamond (see Bright Cut The Metal, pg. 80). This is done after
the metal has been rough cut by the onglette graver. Preferrably a mirror
finish is applied to the metal. To bright cut with the flat graver requires a
certain amount of skill in using the graver and its preparation. (see Graver
Preparation, pg. 25).

MILLIGRAIN TOOL

A milligrain tool is used to outline the metal bordering bead set diamonds. The shaft of the tool is inserted into a graver handle for control. At
the tip is a tiny machined wheel that rotates on an axle between a slit in the
metal. When the wheel is rolled back and forth along a sharp edge of metal
outlining the bright cut, it leaves a decorative line of evenly spaced beads.
This is done only upon request and after all other diamond setting work is
completed. To preserve the beaded design, the milligrain is often applied after the jewelry has been polished.

Fig. 1-13. Milligrain tool inserted into a handle vise.

Fig. 1-14. Tip of a milligrain tool.

MILLIMETER DEGREE GAUGE

A millimeter degree gauge is a frequently used instrument to determine the depth and width of metal, and the size of diamonds. Often a decision must be made pertaining to a diamond fitting into a mounting. By measuring the dimensions of the metal, as compared to the diamond, an accurate accessment can be made. For bead setting purposes, the type of gauge in the figure is appropriate. This gauge is equipped with easy-to-read indexes graduating from $\frac{1}{10}$ millimeter to 12 millimeters.

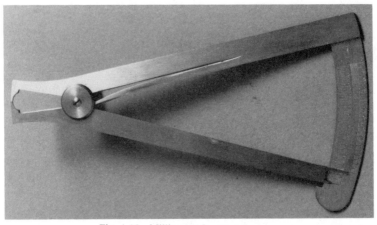

Fig. 1-15. Millimeter degree gauge.

OIL STONES

Oil stones are used primarily to sharpen drills and gravers. They vary in size and shape, but a standard size medium grain stone is most popular for bead setting. Since gravers are repeatedly sharpened, it could be too exhausting to use a fine grain stone. Conversely, a graver sharpened on a coarse grain oil stone will not have a smooth cutting edge. Often the stone is mounted into a low wooden box that is tacked to the top of the workbench. The box controls the overflow of oil from the stone and maintains a fixed position. See Sharpening Gravers on page 30 for proper use of the oil stone.

Fig. 1-16. Oil stones.

POLISHING STONE

A polishing stone is used to polish the bottom of a flat graver tip for bright cutting. A penknife size hard Arkansas stone having the finest grain is preferred. The more it is used, the better it works. As the grain fills with residue (sludge) from oil and dirt, the surface becomes smoother, thereby providing a brighter finish to the flat graver. For that reason the stone should never be cleaned. Using a polishing stone is extensively covered in Section II —Bright Cut The Metal.

Fig. 1-17. Polishing stone.

RUBBER WHEELS

Pumice wheels are used to remove abrasions and smooth metal. The type illustrated in the procedures of this book are ⅝ inch knife edge pumice wheels. They are attached to a ³⁄₃₂ inch shaft and inserted into the flex-shaft machine. The pumice wheel should rotate at a moderate speed and applied to the metal in a brushing manner to avoid gouging the metal. Occasionally the knife edge of the pumice wheel will become rounded from use. It can be sharpened by rotating it against a coarse file. Other methods of removing scratches and file marks from jewelry metal, such as emery paper, at times are difficult due to the small crevices which are inaccessible to the paper.

Larger rubber wheels made of silicon carbide are also used for cleanup work during the final stage of bead setting. Because many surfaces are flat or otherwise massive, a ⅞ inch by ⅛ inch size is recommended. These rubber wheels are use only for areas of the mounting that have not been engraved such as the sides of a plate or undergallery. They are used in a manner similar to that of pumice wheels, but the edge is kept flat rather than sharp.

Fig. 1-18. Rubber wheels (silicon carbide and knife edge pumice)

RING CLAMP

The ring clamp is a handpiece fixture used to hold rings and certain other jewelry for crafting to maintain a steady workpiece and avoid injury. It is especially important to use the ring clamp when drilling or performing other machining operations. A common ring clamp is made of a hardwood, rounded at one end and flat at the other end. The matching leather inserts at each end protect the jewelry from being marred. The ring clamp works by two pieces of wood banded together near the center that swivel on a metal rod separating the two. With a ring held between the leather inserts at one end, a wooden wedge is forced into the opposite end causing the ring to be clamped tight.

Fig. 1-19. Ring clamp.

SCRIBER

A scriber is a hardened steel pointed tool having the likeliness of a pencil. It is used to mark the softer precious metals, to engrave border lines, and to denote space between diamonds in the layout phase of the pavé setting procedure. Scribers are handy to have on occasion, but some diamond setters option to use a graver or a point of the dividers to do the same. Rather than search for a scriber at the moment that an engraving is needed, another tool is often elected. This is because a habit is usually developed to use the first available tool that can be adopted to do the job. If a scriber is preferred, one can be made from a broken ³⁄₃₂ inch bur. It need only be ground to a point and secured by a pin vise.

Fig. 1-20. Scriber made from a ³⁄₃₂ inch bur shaft inserted into a pin vise.

WORKBENCH

The workbench should provide a sturdy and comfortable workplace for long periods of confinement. It should be large enough to accommodate the tools of the trade in an accessible area that can be reached from a sitting position. The anatomy of each craftsman varies and so should the workbench. Adjustable chairs are helpful to a point, but the height of the fell tray, bench top, and arm rest are all worthy of consideration. Special care should be taken from the beginning to make sure that the workbench is suitable to the individual.

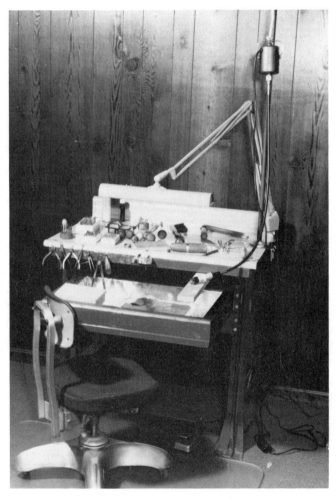

Fig. 1-21. Workbench.

2

Heat Treating Steel

Heat treating is a cycling process of heating and cooling steel to alter its characteristics. It is a highly specialized field in industry but can be done sufficiently to certain types of steel at the workbench. Some common types of steel tools can be made soft in order to file and machine them to specific shapes and then hardened again for durability and effectiveness. Other changes to reverse the metal from a brittle state to improve toughness can also be performed easily with only a torch, pliers and water.

Since the tools used to bead set diamonds require periodic maintenance, a basic knowledge of heat treating steel is necessary. Specifically, beading tools must occasionally be made or reshaped on the premises. Also the cutting tips of gravers often become brittle to a degree that bits of metal break from them thereby preventing a continual cutting action. Conversely, gravers may be too soft to maintain a sharp cutting edge. Many of these problems and more can be corrected with a little experience and awareness of the effects that various temperature ranges have on tool steel.

There are several classifications of steel and hundreds of sub-types. Each is labeled by the type and percentage of alloy content, and requires a specific thermo cycle to heat treat. Some steels, high speed for instance, that contain abundant quantities of an alloy such as tungsten, vanadium, or manganese cannot be heat treated without special equipment and scientific engineering data. The steel that can be heat treated without sophisticated equipment and extensive information is carbon steel.

Steel is a potential tool metal because it has a particular order and bonding of atoms that can be altered by heating and cooling. This orderly arrangement of atoms is called the crystal structure. It can be repeated and reversed by a temperature controlled procedure. Steel is made by a chemical process of combining iron with small amounts of carbon. Neither iron nor carbon by itself is suitable for tool use. When the two elements are heated together at about 1400°F., depending upon the exact percentage of carbon, the crystal structure is in its hardest formation. If allowed to cool slowly the atoms of the structure will dislocate and return to a weaker union. The crystal structure can be trapped in a hard formation by quickly cooling it. Provided there is an ample carbon content, such as carbon tool steel has, the metal can be softened and hardened by varying its temperature within specified time periods.

When tool steel is heated, its color changes at varying temperature ranges. This characteristic of steel allows a craftsman to anneal, harden, and temper the metal without having sophisticated equipment. The color of steel can be used to determine its temperature within a general range of degrees. However, heat colors are affected by lighting in the room that they are observed and one's own perception. In effect, the exact temperature could be perceived as over one hundred degrees difference. Therefore an experienced craftsman will have developed his/her own coloring guide by trial-and-error and more accurately access the proper temperature changes.

ANNEALING

Annealing is a phase of heat treatment that is done to soften steel in order to shape it easily. Previous use of the metal results in its crystal structure being locked in a rigid strain. Annealing relieves the bond to make the steel ductile. Ductility is a relaxed state of steel where it can be hammered thin, drawn into wire, filed, or in other words easily machined. In an annealed formation the bonding between iron and carbon atoms is reduced. Thus, the elements are arranged in their original condition. Before this can occur, the two must first be merged into a uniform whole by heating. Then if allowed to cool slowly the steel will become annealed.

Under ideal conditions the steel being annealed is first placed in a furnace having a pyrometer to measure the temperature and soaked at a constant heat for about two hours. The exact temperature and duration are specified by the carbon and alloy content. For many carbon tool steels the mean temperature is about 1400°F. At that temperature the crystal structure of the iron and carbon is arranged in its most desirable order. Only from that condition can the steel be returned to its original ductile state. This is done by cooling it in the furnace at about 100°F. per hour.

That method is of course too time consuming for a quick maintenance procedure and probably not necessary for most diamond setting purposes. Annealing can be done reasonably well simply by using a pair of pliers to hold the steel over a torch until the steel turns a cherry red color. At that color the metal is about 1400°F. Then it is set aside on a fire-resistant surface for a few minutes until it cools, or until the steel can be placed on a crucible or charcoal block and torched until the desired color appears. To test the anneal try filing the steel. If it is not soft, then try heating the metal to a brighter red or about 1550°F. Remember that this can only be done at the work bench to carbon tool steel, not high speed or other alloy steels. Also the carbon content varies in steels and each type requires a different annealing temperature.

HARDENING

Hardening is necessary to make a steel tool being manufactured or reconditioned capable of machining other metals. Steel that has become intentionally softened by annealing in order to shape it, or accidentally over tempered, will be tough. But it may not be hard enough to serve its purpose as a tool. The steel can be hardened again because of its orderly repeating crystal structure. During the previous heat treating phase of annealing the steel was heated to a temperature where the iron and carbon were combined at their strongest atomic bond. The formation of this crystal structure can be held constant by trapping the elements before they can return to their original position.

All steels contain some amount of carbon as a hardening ingredient. In carbon tool steel the percentage of carbon by weight is 0.6 to 1.7 percent. Steel containing more than 1.7 percent carbon is cast iron. Carbon steel having less than 0.6 percent carbon is increasingly difficult to harden for tool use. Therefore an ideal carbon tool steel to use if hardenability is most important is 0.8 percent carbon tool steel.

The simplest means of hardening steel can be done with only a few basic materials: a propane or gas/oxygen torch; holding pliers; and a container of water. Generally the steel being hardened is first grasped at one end by the pliers and held over the torch. (Most steel tools that are heat treated for diamond setting purposes, such as beading tools and gravers, require handles. For that reason the entire length of the tool does not need to be heated so the tool is held from the handle end). When the steel turns cherry red or about 1400°F, the crystal structure is at its hardest formation.

To keep the crystal structure in a hard formation, or trap the iron and carbon when they are favorably merged, the steel is submerged into water. This is called quenching and must be done immediately. Water will quench steel at about 1000°F per second. Alternate means of quenching are oil and air cooled. These methods are necessary for certain types of steel other than carbon tool steel.

TEMPERING

When steel is quench hardened it is not yet suitable for tool purposes. It will likely be harder than the metal that it is to cut, but not as tough. Quench hardened steel is brittle. It will crack or chip under stress. This is evident in gravers that have been over heated against a grinding wheel and dipped into water during a shaping process. When the quenched graver is used to engrave metal, the extreme cutting tip will be brittle. It will keep breaking and require excessive sharpening. (Water cooling should be done continually during grinding to prevent a graver from over heating, not quench it after over heating). Tempering will have an effect on ductility and hardness. A slight effect on ductility is favorable, and if tempering is done properly the effect on hardness will not be noticeable.

Tempering quench hardened steel is done by reheating it to a temperature between 375° to 550°F. The exact temperature depends on the type of steel and percentage of carbon. Some steels require quenching in water or oil to temper and some must be air cooled. For diamond setting purposes a certain amount of experimenting is usually more feasible than controlled conditions and scientific data. The approximate temperature of the steel can be determined by its color change from yellow, brown, and purple as the temperature rises between 375° to 550°F. Each advance of temperature range toughens the steel more but further reduces the hardness.

FORGING

Forging is a heat treating procedure of shaping steel by hammering or die-striking. It is particularly useful for diamond setting purposes when shaping beading tools. Manufactured steel that has been forged rather than cast is stronger because a finer grain structure is formed. Industrial applications of forging require machine powered presses capable of a force that is unobtainable by hand forging. Diamond setters like the blacksmith can mock the techniques of forging on a smaller scale.

To forge a small steel tool it is first heated to approximately 1900° to 2200°F. At that temperature the steel will turn a bright yellow to white color. The grain will be coarse but will become finer when the steel is hammered. Work should be done swiftly to avoid prolonging the exposure of the steel to such a high temperature. The grain structure could become permanently altered as if it were cast. When the steel reaches the desired heat range it is pliable. Then it can be held by holding pliers to a hardened steel bench block or anvil and hammered to a specific shape. After the steel cools below 1375°F, or as a red glow disappears, the process is repeated until the steel is formed.

3

Graver Preparation

Bead setting requires an extensive use of gravers. Consequently, engraving is an obstacle that if not perfected can confine a diamond setter to performing limited types of diamond setting. Pavé setting certainly cannot be accomplished without the skillful use of gravers. Assuming that a diamond setter can proficiently set diamonds by other means, there is no reason why working with gravers should be such a common impediment. The secret is the preparation of the gravers. A good quality graver, when properly conditioned, is designed to do a significant amount of work. A diamond setter need only maintain its useful condition and simply control it.

In order for a graver to function most effectively and efficiently, it must among other things be controllable. A graver that is too long will likely slip from the workpiece because the thrust cannot be restrained. The graver should offer a good grip and still permit the thumb to brace on the workpiece or fixture. Comfortable handles are important too. A preference of handles varies among the multiple types and sizes similar to the fitting of a glove.

The shape of a graver is also a prerequisite to better engraving. A measure of performance can be improved by grinding it to the most advantageous shape. Whether a graver is selected to raise beads, excavate excess metal, or bright cut, only about one half to one millimeter of the tip's cutting surface does the actual cutting. The remainder of the tip should be ground along the back a short distance. This metal interferes with the visual aspects of work being done, previous work, and prolongs the sharpening process.

Sharpening gravers is an indispensible process that should be done continually. Only a few precise cuts can be made on precious metal between sharpening even with the best of high speed gravers. The method of sharpening the graver, the grain of the oil stone used, the sharpening angle, and cutting angle, all regulate the cutting ability of the graver. This is often a tedious and frustrating task associated with bead setting, and at times a seemingly continuous ordeal. However, the presentation in this segment is designed to lighten the burden significantly.

The laborious efforts of engraving can be overcome by maintaining the useful condition of the gravers. Graver preparation is a three phase process: assembling the graver and handle; grinding the graver to a perfected shape; and sharpening the graver. A graver complete with a handle should accommodate a craftsman in the areas of comfort and control. It should be shaped specifically for its intended purpose. And, a graver must be sharpened routinely so that it will do more physical work than the operator. In effect, the proficiency of bead setting is more predominant in those diamond setters who realize the necessity of tool preparation.

ASSEMBLING GRAVER AND HANDLE

Upon receipt of a new graver, it is normally too long and without a handle. A graver is shortened for control and ground at the handle end in order to be accepted into the handle. After assembly, the graver should be more manageable. It should fit coupled in the palm with the blade extending to the outstretched finger tips. At this size the graver tip is easily maneuverable about the jewelry piece and restrained with the thumb braced against the ring clamp or other fixture.

To shorten the graver, tighten it vertically in a vise with only the section of the handle end to be broken off sticking up. This is usually about one inch. Use a hammer or other blunt tool to strike each side of the metal until it breaks off (see fig. 1-22). A high speed steel graver will be brittle at the handle end and break easily. Gravers made of carbon steel often have to be bent back and forth quite a few times before breaking. If preferred, the excess metal could be ground away rather than broken, but that method is more time consuming.

After a graver is shortened by removing part of the handle end, it will probably not be readily accepted into a handle. The metal will of course be too blunt at that end. The wood handle could crack if the metal is forced into it, especially if the handle has not been previously used. To prevent cracking, a new handle should be drilled at the opening a considerable depth with a one-eighth inch drill (see fig. 1-23). Before attempting to insert the graver into a handle, first grind the handle end of the graver to a size that will allow it to fit without too much force. While grinding keep the metal tapered to preserve its strength (see fig. 1-24).

A graver should fit tightly into a handle. If it is loose there will be less control. Also the extra struggle for control requires unnecessary energy exertion that could result in fatigue. One common method to assemble the graver and handle is to tighten the graver in a vise and tap the handle onto it. Another method is to place the handle on a bench block and tap the graver into it (see fig. 1-25). In either method the insertion should be forced somewhat but just enough to ensure a snug and lasting union.

Fig. 1-22. Shorten a new graver by breaking off a section off the handle end.

Fig. 1-23. Drill a one-eighth inch hole into a new handle.

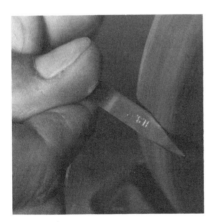

Fig. 1-24. Taper handle end of graver.

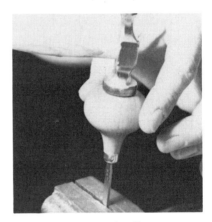

Fig. 1-25. Tap graver handle onto graver.

Eventually gravers will become shortened beyond control after undergoing periodic shaping and sharpening. Because of the expense and attachment to particular tools, the owner/operator genuinely has a difficult time giving them up. When gravers are too short for proper use, the handles can be changed to make the tools longer. Instead of discarding used gravers it is a common practice to change to longer handles, but that presents another problem. After being accustomed to a certain design of handle and then reverting to an alternate, there is always a degree of confusion. This concept is questionable as to its importance because the incidence of chipping diamonds and other damage is seldom fully documented for cause. However, it is known that any change of tooling alters the rhythm of the work being performed.

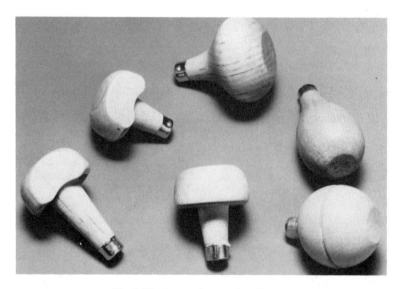

Fig. 1-26. Assorted graver handles.

SHAPING GRAVERS

Gravers are ground to specific shapes depending upon the type of graver and its intended use. Considerations include the necessary strength requirements for particular tasks, accurate sharpening, and precision engraving. The cutting edge must remain untouched but other metal in the immediate vicinity of the tip should taper about three-fourths inch along the back. That entire section will sustain a varying amount of pressure depending on the purpose of the graver. The three basic types of gravers used to bead set diamonds as illustrated in this book are the round, onglette, and flat gravers. Each of these are scheduled to a special shape that pertains to their unique purpose.

Observing the illustrations in figure 1-27, notice the shapes of the three gravers: the round graver is particularly rigid at the tip compared to the others because it is frequently used with much more force; the onglette graver requires some strength but is narrow at the tip for continual efficient sharpening. This shape also permits visibility and clearance from other areas of jewelry during cutting procedures; lastly, flat gravers used for bright cutting necessitate even more unobstructing features and less strength than that required of onglette gravers. The sides are ground as close as possible to the cutting edge to remain clear of beadwork while cutting adjacent to the diamond. Therefore, when shaping gravers some sacrifices will have to be compromised to obtain the most favorable advantage for each type of graver.

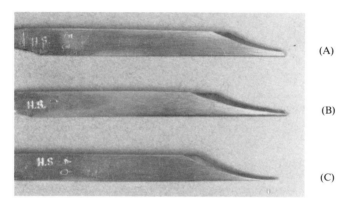

(A)

(B)

(C)

Fig. 1-27. Shaping specifications of gravers. (A) round graver, (B) onglette graver, (C) flat graver.

Grinding a graver is a detailed and time-consuming task if done properly. Keep in mind that the tool steel has been heat treated to strict specifications. Friction between the graver and grinding wheel will cause heat to build up very quickly. There is a tendency of the heat to radiate to the tip. The metal, being thin there, will burn quickly even if it is not touched by the grinding wheel. If the metal is overheated it will anneal, making the graver impossible to keep sharp. Revising the original heat treatment to the metal could be awkward using the limited equipment found in most jewelry shops. Shaping the graver is expected to consume a considerable amount of time, but the time spent is a good investment in the long run.

The recommended graver shaping process, being preventive in nature, is to grind the graver from the tip along the back using brief brushing strokes, and applying slight pressure against the grinding wheel (see fig. 1-28). Passing the graver against the grinding wheel is called the feed. The feed should be at a rate that the graver will endure no more than one second of machining from the tip to about three-fourth inch along the back, and it should be continuous in that the graver is constantly moving. Permitting any section of the metal to remain in contact with the grinding wheel, even briefly, will cause the section to overheat.

Fig. 1-28. Graver shaping.

In addition to the feed rate, to avoid heat buildup the metal should also be immediately submerged into a container of water after each stroke against the grinding wheel. The water is placed next to the grinding machine for easy access. Carelessly overheating the metal then quenching it into water will cause it to become brittle. Being brittle, the graver tip will break during each cut. To remedy this, the metal will have to be tempered (see Tempering, pg. 23). Remember that water is used to prevent the graver from overheating, not to cool it after it overheats.

SHARPENING GRAVERS

Sharpening a graver is a simpler task, although time consuming overall because it is a recurring necessity. Normally only a few sharp cuts can be made between each time the graver is sharpened. However, the act itself is only a matter of briskly stroking the graver back and forth across an oil stone four or five times. There are particulars to be presented here concerning the sharpening and cutting angles, direction of strokes, and minor problems that may arise.

Using an oil stone is a basic mechanical process that the reader has probably experienced on several occasions prior to becoming a diamond setter. However, the crude and free style manner in which the knife is sharpened is not applicable to that of sharpening a graver. Sharpening a graver requires much more precision and accuracy because of its purpose. Preferably a medium grain stone is used. A fine grain or "hard" stone is suitable but slow cutting. Using it becomes monotonous after awhile since the graver will be sharpened several times. A coarser grain stone will cut more efficiently but leaves a rough cutting edge at the tip of the graver. It is especially important when bright cutting that the flat graver is evenly sharpened. Also cutting oil should be applied to the oil stone. The oil will cause the ground metal to float thereby leaving the stone's grain open for effective sharpening.

A graver should be held at approximately 45° to 55° angle to the oil stone when it is being sharpened. At this angle the graver tip will more readily remove the metal when engraving. A higher sharpening angle will not cut as well, and at a lower sharpening angle the graver will have a tendency to chip at the cutting edge. Each of these factors are related to the angle that the graver is held when it is actually cutting the metal. These angles are discussed in the pertaining segments of Section II — The Bead Setting Procedure. By experimenting with the sharpening angle and the cutting angle, a craftsman can determine what is most comfortable and proficient.

To obtain an even cutting edge across the tip of a graver, it has to be held steady in order to control any side movement or slanting while it is being sharpened. One good habit to develop as a measure of control is to grasp the sides of the graver near the tip between the thumb and forefinger (see figure 1-29). This will help to guide the graver and keep it from tilting to either side while it is being sharpened. Otherwise, the tip will become rounded. By curling the remaining fingers around the handle, the direction and proper sharpening angle of the graver can be applied to the oil stone. For best results press down on the forward stroke across the length of the oil stone and release pressure but slide on the back stroke. The graver should sharpen after four or five repetitions.

Fig. 1-29. Graver sharpening.

Test the sharpness of the graver by placing the tip at a low angle against a soft metal such as brass or silver. (Some diamond setters use their own thumb nail). It should stick without sliding forward freely. If it does not adhere then, it may not be sharp enough, or, sometimes a burr of metal has developed at the tip. This burr is common and can be removed easily by lightly jabbing the tip into a block of wood attached to the front edge of the workbench. If the burr is persistent and cannot be easily removed, then the graver metal may have become annealed, probably during the shaping process. In this case it will have to be heat treated.

4

Making A Beading Tool

Making a beading tool, or reshaping a worn beading tool, is also a usual and recurring necessity when bead setting. There are two means of doing this. Each is an option that involves the application of heat treatment (see Heat Treating, pg. 21). One procedure is to first anneal the tool. After it cools it can be shaped with the use of a beading tool plate. Then it is hardened and tempered. The other procedure is to forge the concave tip into the beading tool (see Forging, pg. 24). Forging also requires the use of a beading tool plate and heat treatment but the procedure is a little different.

Although either of the two options to reshape a beading tool works very well, each has advantages and disadvantages. For practical purposes both procedures are presented in this segment. The first option is to reshape an annealed beading tool, and the second is to reshape a beading tool by forging. After considering both options, the individual may choose which is more preferred for his or her own style.

OPTION NO. 1 — BY HEAT TREATMENT

Step 1. Select a carbon tool steel rod about one-eighth inch in diameter and two inches long. Only carbon tool steel can be heat treated at the workbench (see Heat Treating, pg. 21). A worn domestic beading tool is preferred, but a similar section can be cut from the handle end of a needle file. If a nee-

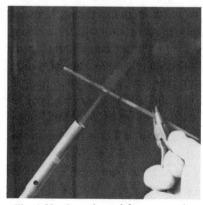

Fig. 1-30. Anneal metal for easy sawing.   Fig. 1-31. Cool metal on heat resistant plate.

32

dle file or other carbon metal is to be used, anneal an area of the metal about two inches from the end (see fig. 1-30). After it cools, the metal should be soft enough to saw through (see fig. 1-32).

Step 2. Grind or file a cone shape at one end beginning about one fourth inch from the end. This will be the tip. It should taper evenly around the rod to the extreme tip. The metal may have to be annealed at this area again if it is to be filed. The taper can be formed using a grinding machine by turning the rod continually while grinding (see fig. 1-33).

Fig. 1-32. Saw metal at annealed area.

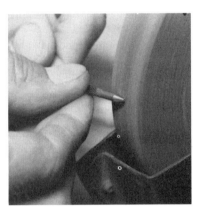

Fig. 1-33. Grind one end of the cut off section to a taper.

Step 3. File the point of the tip even and at a right angle to the shaft (see fig. 1-34). The concave that forms the bead will be stamped there so file just enough to flatten the point. The result should be a circular flat area centered at the tip of the rod that is the diameter of the bead to be formed.

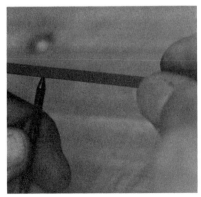

Fig. 1-34. File a flat surface at tapered end.

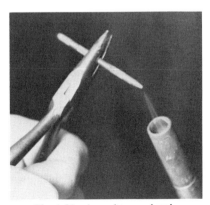

Fig. 1-35. Anneal tapered end.

Step 4. Anneal the tip of the beading tool to prepare it for stamping. The entire tool does not need to be annealed. To do this heat the metal to about 1400°F. It can be heated on a charcoal block or crucible, or use pliers to hold it over a torch (see fig. 1-35). The metal will glow a red color at that temperature.

Step 5. Let the tool cool by itself on a fire resistant surface for about three or four minutes, or until it can be handled (see fig. 1-36). After cooling, the metal should be soft and ready for stamping.

Fig. 1-36. Place the metal on a heat resistant surface to cool slowly.

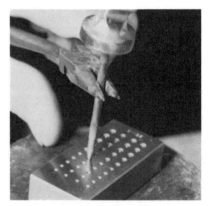

Fig. 1-37. Hold the rod firmly to tap the tip onto the beading tool plate.

Step 6. Select an appropriate size bead on the beading tool plate, then put the plate on the bench block. Be sure that the bench block is on a sturdy area of the workbench. The best location is usually directly over a bench leg. Test the placement by tapping on the beading tool with a chasing hammer. If there is a bounce or vibration, then use another location.

Step 7. Set the tip of the beading tool on the selected bead and perpendicular to the beading tool plate. Grasp the mid-section of the beading tool shaft with a pair of pliers that have secure gripping jaws. Use the other hand to hold the hammer. A chasing hammer or similar light weight hammer should be used because too much force on the beading tool could cause the shaft to bend.

Step 8. Swiftly strike once straight down onto the bead (see fig. 1-37). If the concave does not form perfectly at the tip of the beading tool the first time, it will have to be annealed again. This is because pounding hardens the metal. Additional attempts to form a concave tip without reannealing could result in a broken bead on the beading tool plate. Some adjustment can be made by filing if the concave is formed well but not centered at the tip.

Step 9. To harden the tip of a reshaped beading tool, grasp the end of the tool with pliers and hold the tip over a torch flame (see fig. 1-38). Only the tip needs to be hardened. When the color of the metal turns red it will be about 1400°F. At that time quickly drop the tool into a container of water (see fig. 1-39). This will quench the metal.

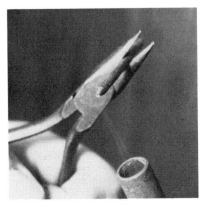

Fig. 1-38. Heat the beading tool tip for quench hardening.

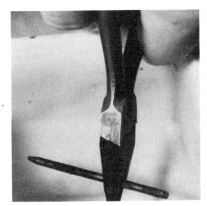

Fig. 1-39. Water quench the beading tool.

If the metal is not hard after that, then try heating it to a higher temperature or brighter red color then quench it again. The quicker the metal is transferred from the flame to the water, the harder the metal will be. There is no need to temper a beading tool after hardening.

OPTION NO. 2 — BY FORGING

Making a beading tool by forging is in many ways similar to the previous method but there are a few exceptions. One difference is that the cavity of the beading tool is formed while the tip is red hot or hotter. It is not annealed first. The beading tool is taken directly from the flame of the torch to the beading tool plate. Extra caution should be observed to control the hot beading tool when it is held by the pliers. There is a danger that it could fly when hit by the hammer. Otherwise the beading tool is set, held, and stricken in the same manner as the previous method. In both methods after the bead cavity is formed the metal is quench hardened. Before attempting to forge the tip of a beading tool, the forging segment on page 24 should be reviewed in order to understand the principles involved.

SECTION II

The Bead Setting Procedure

Introduction

Among the many procedures of diamond setting none is more basic than bead setting, yet it represents more experience to perfect than any other. Completing the procedure in an artistic style requires the craftsman to become a perfectionist at basic diamond setting skills of using tools, cutting bearings, securing diamonds, etc. Less involved procedures such as needle point and prong setting compel a limited expansion of resourcefulness and imagination. Other advanced procedures are increasingly complex but also restricted to specific resolutions. Conclusively, bead setting as opposed to other types of diamond setting is an accomplished skill that is acquired after a greater number of prerequisite skills are obtained. The rewards of self satisfaction and gratification are great. No other type of diamond setting offers a diamond setter the freedom to plan a layout of diamonds on a blank plate of metal and to possess total decision making control from beginning to end.

Bead setting is the most flexible of diamond setting procedures in that it allows for the diamonds being set into a mounting to have various arrangement possibilities. Perhaps its greatest application is that of remounting diamonds. A customer's collection of previously set diamonds, regardless of number and size range, can be remounted into an extensive assortment of mountings. A large percentage of the average retail jeweler's service business is derived from customers who turn in some, or all, of their jewelry to have the diamonds remounted into a single piece of jewelry. The diamonds may vary in any number of sizes and cuts, and still be compatible to an unlimited selection of mountings.

Jewelry manufacturers are somewhat reluctant to mass produce diamond jewelry that must be bead set because of the labor expense. Bead setting normally involves more labor time, where pin point or prong setting is much more efficient. There is however, at this time, a trend in jewelry fashion to produce increasing quantities of bead set jewelry, but it remains to be on a limited scale. Some major production manufacturers favoring pavé designs are introducing mountings that appear to be bead set but are actually prong set. To compensate the diamonds are seated directly on the surface of the metal. In these designs the prongs are filed down close to the girdles of the diamonds and the plate to appear as beads rather than prongs. It is an effective means to accomplish a resemblance of bead setting, but still restricted to a particular assortment of diamonds. The idea is hardly practical for the majority of remounts because the customer's collection of diamonds is not likely to be compatible to a mounting that was designed for a specific size range of diamonds.

Bead setting defined in its most basic application is to set a diamond into the surface of a solid plate of metal. An elaborate description would assume that the center of the metal is first located and drilled. Then the hole is excavated by a tapered bore, and a bearing is cut that extends below the surface. When the diamond is tightly seated into the bearing, a number of burrs are formed from the surrounding metal to secure it. Afterwards, the bordering metal is engraved to enhance the diamond. This process sounds basic enough, and it is. However, each phase of the procedure, being basic to the aspects of other diamond setting procedures, becomes intensely involved with its own outline of applications and alternative measures.

This section is organized to describe each phase of the bead setting procedure in sequence. It begins with determining where the diamonds should be set, and concludes with bright cutting the metal after the diamonds are set. Do's and don'ts of each phase are included as well as alternative measures and problem solving techniques. These basic skills are then applied to a series of actual bead setting situations that are presented in the following section.

1

Inspect The Mounting

Jewelry mountings differ in quality and workmanship as much as any other manufactured product. Preliminary visual and mechanical inspections of the mounting are made to determine its compatibility for diamond setting. There are a number of features to consider: foremost the metal has to be of a gauge that the diamonds can be properly set into it without falling through; if the mounting is a ring, the plate metal should be high enough that after the diamonds are set the culets will not protrude into the finger area; an early determination should also be made concerning the strength of the undergallery supporting the plate metal; and there should be adequate space for all of the diamonds to be set. A critical evaluation of the mounting upon receipt could prevent hours of frustration.

When the diamonds are bead set they are seated below the surface of the metal. It is conceivable then that the metal at those locations will become thinner. Working with a plate of metal that is no thicker than the depth that a bearing should be cut may prove inept. The diamond will, of course, fall through. Ideally the metal should be at least three-fourth millimeter thick for setting diamonds up to .04 ct or .05 ct. Larger diamonds require more metal. To check the metal for thickness do not rely exclusively on a visual inspection from a side view. This is helpful but could be deceiving because the edge of a plate is commonly built up more than the center area (see fig. 2-1). Some causes of this result from the casting process or from the removal of too much metal when the casting was filed, emeried, and prepolished. An accurate way to test the metal for true thickness is with the use of a millimeter gauge (see fig. 2-2).

Fig. 2-1.   Illustrates how the actual thickness of a plate
could be deceiving if the metal is built up at
the edge.

41

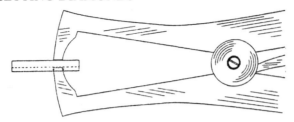

Fig. 2-2.   Use a millimeter degree gauge to measure the
thickness of a plate.

The next inspection concerns the person who will ultimately wear the
ring. This is to determine whether or not the diamonds can be set into the
metal without having the culets protrude into the finger area. Discomfort to
the wearer is a justifiable reason to reject the craftsmanship of the completed work. Also it is a common cause of diamonds being chipped if and
when the ring is sized. (During sizing the ring is pounded on a steel mandrel,
the diamonds could become chipped or forced out of the setting.) A de-
cisive inspection in this matter could be made in either or both of two ways:
one way is to hold the diamond to the side of the plate where it is to be set
(see fig. 2-3). With the diamond lowered to a level where it will be seated,
the extension of the culet can be seen; the other method is to use a millimeter degree gauge to measure the diamond from its culet to its table facet
and apply that measurement to the mounting. Using the latter method, an
allowance is given for the distance from the surface of the plate to the proposed depth of the bearing.

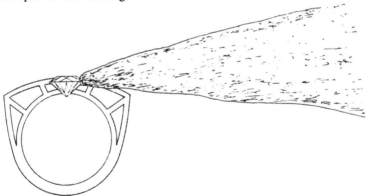

Fig. 2-3.   Shows a diamond being held with bees wax
to the side of a plate. This is done to determine if the culet will extend into the finger
area when the diamond is lowered to a level
where it will ultimately be seated.

Another inspection deals with the strength of the mounting. The strength of the mounting is directly related to setting the diamonds because of the force and pressure that will be applied to the mounting. Some of the major faults to check for are extended spans of metal between braces of the undergallery, weak or imperfect bridging supports, an a fragile ring shank that will bend or collapse under the pressure exerted to bead set the diamonds (see fig. 2-4). If any of these conditions are apparent, then the plate that the diamonds will be set into will have to be supported with diamond setters cement.

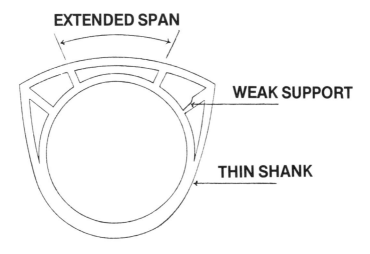

Fig. 2-4.   Shows some major faults to check pertaining to the strength of a ring.

One final inspection is to see that there is enough space on the plate for the diamonds to set. Diamond setters should not assume that diamonds selected by an outside source for a particular mounting will always fit. Bead setting often involves setting a large number of diamonds into a tight formation. The decision to assign the precise placement of a large quantity of diamonds should always involve the opinion of the craftsman who is going to do the diamond setting. Assume, for example, a hypothetical situation where an authoritative figure wants a cluster of diamonds to be set close together into a dome plate. The supervisor first devises a plan to determine how many diamonds can possibly be set into the plate. The diamonds are selected and placed table facet down, girdle-to-girdle on the plate. When the task is completed, the selected number of diamonds and the mounting are given to the diamond setter for setting. An experienced diamond setter would have known beforehand that when diamonds are set down into a dome plate they tend to join closer (see fig. 2-5). In a case such as this if the diamond setter does not personally check to see if there is enough space, the diamonds will overlap each other when the bearings are cut.

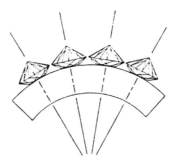

Fig. 2-5.   Shows that diamonds layed out on a dome plate join closer after they are set down into the plate.

Inspecting the mounting prior to actual diamond setting is a brief but all-important preliminary step. Problems ranging from diamonds being set insecurely to total disaster can be avoided. Rightfully this is a task that should be undertaken by the diamond setter rather than accept the assumptions of others.

2

Design A Layout

Bead setting diamonds into a mounting for the most pleasing arrangement is seldom done by randomly distributing the diamonds. Advanced planning is necessary to place the diamonds where they will be presented to the fullest advantage to enhance the jewelry. This is an important phase of bead setting that demands accuracy. Anything less could have an adverse effect, and possibly disrupt the remainder of the procedure. Very little tolerance is acceptable because the procedure will begin to take form at this time. Once a design is devised, often by trial and error, it is transcribed to a layout. A layout is the diamond setter's blueprint. It is a sketch engraved on a mounting to show the size, locations, and borders where diamonds are to be set. The engravings may elaborately consist of arcs, circles, and lines, or only brief tick marks. Broadly speaking, the features of a layout depend upon the shape of the jewelry and the characteristics of the diamonds.

Often the placement of diamonds is obvious or dictated by someone else. In the latter case this phase would be simplified. But the experienced diamond setter might view it as a burden knowing that the decision could have a detrimental effect during a later phase of the procedure. For example, an uncompromising customer may strongly suggest that her eight diamonds, all being equal size and absolutely no sentimental value, be set into a round plate. The diamond setter must reluctantly proceed after advising that seven diamonds will have a greater effect than eight. (A configuration of seven equal size diamonds having six surrounding one in the center can be set girdle-to-girdle and appear as a single large diamond). Had the experience and foresight of the diamond setter not been neglected, the customer's diamonds would have been displayed to the fullest advantage and at less cost.

The design of jewelry frequently suggests the placement of diamonds. Generally diamonds will seem to belong in certain areas. Larger diamonds will be located in the center areas or at the wide end of tapered plates, and smaller diamonds at the narrow end. This is obvious but the task can become confusing because other sections, such as a straight bar of metal, should contain equal size diamonds in order to make their appearance effective there. Other designated areas could be curvatures and metal formed to resemble fancy shapes like marquis, ovals, pears, etc. Many of these fea-

45

tures may be included in the total design of a single mounting. Planning a logical distribution of the diamonds to the best advantage offers an expression of creativity. A successful layout requires that the diamond setter be experienced in the matter in order to know beforehand what difficulties could arise as the work progresses to each area.

Other characteristics of the diamonds, besides the size, which was already discussed, also play an important role in determining where to set them. Some sacrifice may be optioned to place the highest quality diamonds where they will highlight the jewelry. Lower quality diamonds are best presented in less conspicuous areas. Furthermore, diamonds being of the same cut are best grouped together whenever possible. This will promote a consistant order of refraction from the diamonds. In effect, the quality of a diamond should also be considered when planning a layout.

Unless a diamond setter is setting a single diamond into a pre-drilled or obvious location, a certain amount of compromising is undertaken. This is a preliminary phase of bead setting. Before drilling the first hole, a minimal amount of time should be taken to foresee the result. A conflict between experience, design of the jewelry, and characteristics of the diamonds will have to be resolved. Each of these should be considered when deciding where the most effective location is for each diamond to be set. An experienced diamond setter will know in advance what problems could arise in a given situation. The design of the jewelry will limit some decision making, and the separation of diamonds by size and quality could expand the enhancement possibilities.

The process of designing a layout depends upon a number of factors. One is the experience of the craftsman. This is in regards to how much information is needed on a plate in order to recognize the location of each diamond that is to be set. Sometimes only a few marks on the metal are all that is necessary to begin the diamond setting procedure. Any adjustments that might be necessary are made along the way. Another factor is the symmetrics of the mounting, and the size and number of diamonds. In the case of a symmetric configuration the layout can be simplified by locating center lines on the plate and laying out the diamonds on those lines. A third consideration is a freeform type of mounting where center lines either cannot be used, or the diamond setter chooses an alternate means of marking the plate. Each method of designing a layout mentioned is illustrated in this segment on the same plate in order to show the differences between them.

DESIGNING A SYMMETRIC LAYOUT

A symmetric configuration is the easiest design to lay out. There is a certain amount of trial and error using the dividers until exact centers can be

located. After the center lines are found the remainder of the process is rou-
tine. The greatest advantage to this layout method is that the design can be
made with such accuracy that very few adjustments have to be made during
the remainder of the diamond setting procedure.

The first engravings of a symmetric design are done to find the center
line of the plate. This will serve as a reference from where all other engravings are based. To find the center line of a symmetric plate such as the one
represented in the series of figure 2-6 two reference points are needed — one
at each end of the plate. Adjust the dividers from the outside edge of directly opposite sides near either end to a distance just short enough to cross two
arcs on the plate (see fig. 2-6). The exact location of the beginning pivoting
point at each end is arbitrary, but the second arc must begin at an equal distance from the end. Then repeat that phase to the other end of the plate to
find the other reference point. A straight line bisecting the plate is engraved
through the two resulting cross points. The center point of the plate is found
by trial and error by pivoting the dividers from each end of the plate at the
center line until the arcs meet using the same divider adjustment. Other
symmetric points can likewise be found by further dividing the plate.

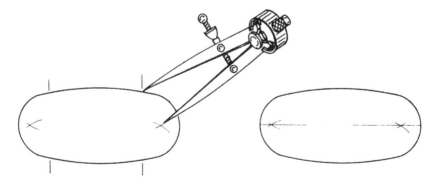

Fig. 2-6. Shows the process of locating the center line
of a plate.

A circle having the diameter of the diamond to be set at each center
point is engraved by the dividers at the pertaining center points (see fig. 2-
7). All drilling, boring, and bearing cutting is maintained within those circles. To avoid misjudgments during the layout, subsequent center points
should be encircled before laying out additional center points. In this manner checks can be made by placing the diamonds on the circles before pro-
ceeding to the next. Also equal spacing can be ensured by working toward the ends of the plate.

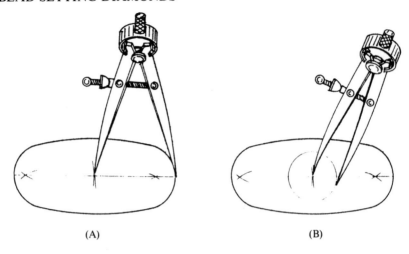

(A)   (B)

Fig. 2-7.   (A) Shows the center point of the plate
located by trial and error from each end of
the plate.
(B) A circle is engraved around the center
point to represent the diamond that will be
set there.

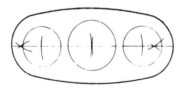

Fig. 2-8.   Shows a symmetric layout for three diamonds that will be set into an oval plate.

DESIGNING A FREEFORM LAYOUT

The design of a freeform layout is developed by eyeing the location and
spacing of each diamond. Dividers are used but only after the center points
are defined. It is a process that involves temporarily placing the diamonds
exactly where they will be set, engraving border lines between the diamonds,
and marking the center points of the diamonds between those border lines.
A graver or scriber is used to make most of the engravings while the diamonds are laid out on the plate.

The initial steps of a freeform layout are to determine exactly where each diamond is to be set. First warm the mounting just enough to apply a thin film of bees wax on the setting areas. Do not allow the mounting to get too hot. Over heating can cause solder joints to unfasten, distortion of the mounting, or distempering. A Bunsen burner, lighter or match will suffice. Then place each diamond via its table facet on the location where it will be set. Use bees wax tapered to a point for handling diamonds, or use tweezers, to place the diamonds onto the mounting (see fig. 2-9). They will adhere to the wax film and can be shifted to proper spacing without easily falling off the plate. Try using a flat graver to gently press on the culet of a diamond for better adherence between its table and the wax on the mounting (see fig. 2-10).

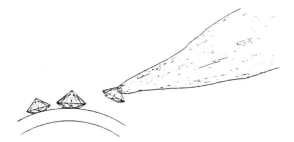

Fig. 2-9. Shows bees wax (option: tweezers) being used to place diamonds on a plate.

Fig. 2-10. Shows a flat graver (option) being used to gently press a diamond into the wax on a plate.

There will be a considerable amount of shifting among the diamonds until a selective order is acquired. Equal amounts of surface metal should be seen between the diamonds to signify proper spacing. Perceive in the plan an acknowledgement that the diamonds being laid out on an elevated plane at the girdle level will actually set closer when lowered to a bearing level. Recall a previous phase how diamonds laid out on a dome plate will tend to join closer together after seated into the metal. Also, when diamonds are too close to the edge of the plate they could end up being set sticking through the edge. Experience is the most valuable asset to foresee the result of the layout from this early stage. Regardless, a cause and effect attitude toward all phases of bead setting will minimize or avoid problems through the procedure.

When confident that there are no further alterations of any significance to make, border markings are engraved between and around the diamonds. These engravings are scratches on the metal just deep enough to remain visible after the diamonds and film of bees wax are removed. Do this while the diamonds are still intact on the mounting using a scriber or onglette graver (see fig. 2-11). An onglette graver is useful for this purpose because of its ability to penetrate between diamonds that are spaced close together. Another benefit of the onglette graver is that it can engrave marks on the plate with little effort. Using an awkward tool or excessive force could jerk the mounting at times causing some diamonds to relocate or fall off. The engravings will range from nothing more than tiny tick marks to complete and distinct border lines that define exact locations. This is a matter of availability of space on the metal, experience, and necessity. When the diamonds are removed, some sort of notation should remain on the metal that the diamond setter can refer to when setting the diamonds.

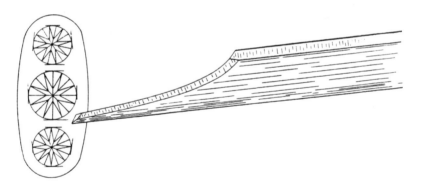

Fig. 2-11. Shows an onglette graver (option: scriber) engraving border markings between and around diamonds.

Before removing the diamonds a tin (pill box size container) is prepared to store and keep them separated when other work is being done. Melted bees wax in it will ensure that the diamonds remain intact (see pg. 165, fig. 4-42). To prepare the tin for this purpose first place a small amount of bees wax in it to be melted. Then grasp the rim via pliers and hold it over a low and consistant flame until the wax melts. Keep the tin level at all times to avoid spilling hot wax, and to allow an even coat of wax to melt on the bottom. When the wax melts place the tin on a level, heat resistant surface and extinguish the flame. After several seconds submerge it into water momentarily or until the wax cools completely. Then carve an enlarged sketch on the wax to include the featured designs of the mounting where the diamonds will be set. The diamonds will later be removed from the mounting and placed on the corresponding locations in the wax. A tin is also a good idea because if work is interrupted it can be closed and placed aside with the diamonds secured in place on the wax carving.

The diamonds are removed from the mounting carefully one at a time. As each diamond is removed the center of its location is marked using a round graver. These center point marks will be referred to later when drilling. To do this, working with one diamond at a time, first place the tip of the graver adjacent to the girdle of the diamond. Focus on a center location of the diamond on the plate without shifting your eyes to follow the diamond when it is moved away. Then nudge the diamond to the side just enough to place the tip of the graver into the metal where the center of the diamond was (see fig. 2-12). The graver need only make a small indentation at this time. As the center of each diamond is marked that diamond is placed on its assigned location of the sketch in the tin before going on to the next diamond.

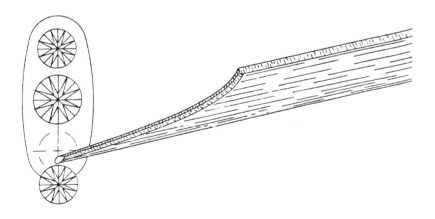

Fig. 2-12. Shows the use of a round graver to nudge a
diamond aside while making a mental note
of the center point and marking it.

After all inside borders and center points are engraved and the diamonds are placed on their corresponding locations in a tin, the outside border lines, if applicable, are engraved. This is done to ensure that a distinct and uniform bright cut can be made later between the diamonds and the edge of the plate. To engrave an edge border, first adjust the dividers to that distance. With one point of the dividers sliding along the outside edge and following the contour, the other point engraves a border on the plate (see fig. 2-13). Bearings for the diamonds that are set along the edge are cut tangent to that border.

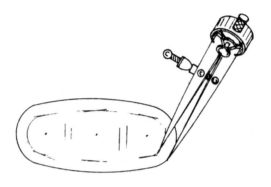

Fig. 2-13. Use dividers to engrave a border that follows the contour of the plate.

The completed layout is a mechanical drawing engraved in the mounting. It shows exactly where holes are to be drilled, and likewise guides all boring, bearing cutting, raising beads, and engraving activities. A diamond setter should be able to look at the layout and visualize any problems that could arise throughout each phase of the bead setting procedure. Also, a diamond setter should from experience be able to foresee every detail of the finished work even before the first hole is drilled.

3

Drill The Holes

Drilling holes correctly is a basic skill of diamond setting. More definitive it is an essential phase of bead setting that precedes taper boring. The purpose of holes is twofold: primarily they enable and regulate the direction of boring burs; secondly, holes provide an exit for dirt removal later when the jewelry is cleaned. Although it appears to be a less complicated task by the layman, precision drilling demands a knowledge of the drill as a tool and expertise in its use.

INDENT CENTER POINTS

Holes are drilled through a plate precisely at the center point where each diamond will be set. The center points engraved during the layout should be notched just enough to make depressions in the metal that will keep the drill from slipping off center. To do this push the tip of a round graver into each center mark at a low angle and scoop or pick a tiny chip of metal from the plate. Pinhead size depressions should result in the plate to serve as starter holes for the drill. This was not done during the layout as each diamond was removed because it requires a forceful intrusion into the metal. Although the diamonds adhere to the wax film on the mounting, the sudden relief of thrust to the graver could cause it to slip and dislocate some diamonds.

HOW A DRILL WORKS

A straight shank twist drill functions as it does because of its unique design. The main features are the *shank, lands, cutting lips, margins, body,* and *flutes* (see fig. 2-14). As the drill turns, metal is cut by cutting lips of the two lands. The cutting lips extend from the center line of the drill at an angle of 59° each to form a 118°-drill point. The average lip clearance angle is between 12° to 15°. To little lip clearance will inhibit cutting and cause the drill to burn. A drill having an excessive lip clearance is too thin at the cutting lip. The cutting edges will easily chip when the drill is used. Margins prevent friction because the distance between them is the largest diameter of the body. Flutes that spiral along the body permit coolants to flow to the point when it is deep into the metal. At the same time metal scrap is brought to the surface.

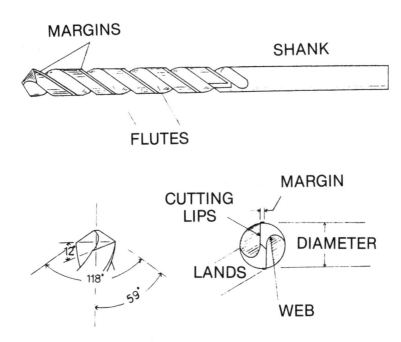

Fig. 2-14. Shows the workings of a twist drill.

DRILLING HOLES

Under normal circumstances all the holes should be drilled in repetition using the same drill before doing any further work. Unless any of the diamonds to be set are considerably less than .01 ct most holes can be drilled using an approximate NO. 65 or .035-inch twist drill. Larger drills remove too much metal, possibly weakening some thinner plates, and smaller drills tend to break too easily. Larger drills are recommended when drilling through thick plates to set larger diamonds. By drilling all the holes before advancing to the next phase, tool changing will be reduced. Also it is easier to assimilate all the holes to equally follow the contour of the mounting because there is less interruption.

SUMMARY

The fundamentals of bead setting described in this section are the building blocks of pavé setting. Successful completion of each phase is dependent upon the accuracy of its preceeding phase. Careful planning and foresight have been stressed to be conceptual prerequisites that are most predominant in pavé setting. Now, assuming that the diamond setter is mechanically inclined and possesses a sufficient degree of perception, there should be no difficulty in employing the previous outline of skills. Referral to these attributes, although subliminal at times, is a continual necessity.

Given that a skill has been acquired to bead set one diamond properly, then there is no reason why several diamonds cannot similarly be set adjacently. Thus, the diamond setter has a reserve of skills to set diamonds in the most classical manner of pavé style. By adhering to the logical order of events step by step, as illustrated here, a structural foundation can be achieved for the bead setting applications found in the following section.

SECTION III

Bead Setting Applications

Introduction

The objectives of this section is to apply bead setting to actual practice. In the previous section the general procedure of bead setting was broken down into phases. Each phase was shown to be dependent upon the success of its subsequent phase. Now that process is pictorially illustrated in a variety of situations beginning with fundamental bead settings, then expands in detail to include setting diamonds into configurations that resemble fancy shapes. Finally the section concludes with bead setting diamonds into rows and curves. The obvious progression of steps is included as well as the finer, noteworthy details that are particular to each application. Upon completion of this section, the diamond setter will have obtained a comprehensive knowledge of bead setting techniques that can be referred to at the workbench.

The first couple applications are concerned with the fundamentals of the bead setting procedure. The procedure is applied respectively to a star setting and a square plate. Designs such as these require basic bead setting skills but emphasize the engraving aspects of the procedure. A diamond is set into a mounting to be displayed, but the mounting may enhance the diamond as well. The diamond setter should learn that besides securing a diamond, the design of the jewelry also plays an important role in the outcome.

Additional applications gradually introduce more complexity as they progress to a basic triangle plate and other geometric shapes. Eventually illustrations of bead setting multiple diamonds into a marquis shaped plate demonstrate that smaller diamonds can be arranged to resemble a single larger and fancier diamond. Exercises learned during those progressive applications are designed to build a thorough program of bead setting.

The section concludes with bead setting a series of diamonds into a row and a curve. These are advanced versions of the basic single diamond settings that are applied later to the final section of pavé setting. Unique layout schemes, beading arrangements, bright cuts, and special effects are presented. The diamond setter is encouraged to use those ideas to develop others. After concluding these applications the diamond setter, given the time and opportunity, should be prepared to confront any bead setting task.

1

Star Setting

A star setting is prevalent in jewelry that has a spacious area of metal such as a signet ring, charm, or watchcase. A single diamond is set into each setting, but if preferred several star settings may be independently included in a given area. The diamond is centered between a number of bright cut engravings that conventionally represent the points of a star. When the design is engraved, as prescribed, the entire plate will appear to be transpired by the seemingly endless extensions of the star points. Therefore, only one diamond and star setting is necessary. Other convenient reasons for applying a star setting are that the customer may possess, or wish to purchase, only one diamond. Also, a manufacturer might find it practical for pricing purposes to furnish a single diamond to be set into the jewelry piece. Although a star setting is confined to the use of one diamond, and it has no border, the format of setting the diamond is basic to other bead setting procedures. The design is introduced in this beginning application to demonstrate the importance and effects of engraving as a task of the diamond setter.

STEP 1 — INSPECT THE MOUNTING
(Fig. 3-1)

(a) Measure the thickness of the metal with a millimeter degree gauge. Be sure that the diamond can be set into the plate without falling through when the bearing is cut.

(b) The plate should be high enough that after the diamond is set its culet will not protrude into the finger area.

(c) Determine the strength of the ring shank and the undergallery that supports the plate metal.

(d) Check to see that there is enough space on the plate to set the diamond and to cut the engravings.

STEP 2 — DESIGN A LAYOUT
(Fig. 3-2)

Place the ring on a mandrel to find the center lines. Use a scriber to engrave center lines on the plate in perspective to the lines on the mandrel (see fig. 3-2). Do not engrave the metal more than necessary to distinguish the center lines. The length of the lines should be slightly longer than the diameter of the diamond being set. Scratches are difficult to remove from the surface of a signet ring after the diamond is set. Use dividers to check for accuracy by adjusting the points from the ends and sides of the plate to the center point.

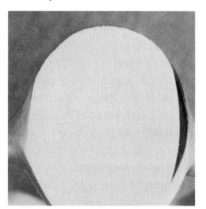

Fig. 3-1. Signet ring.

Fig. 3-2. Engraving center lines in perspective to the lines on a mandrel.

STEP 3 — DRILL THE HOLE
(Fig. 3-3)

Use a round graver to cut a small depression into the metal at the center point. This will serve as a starter hole to keep the drill on center. Drill the hole perpendicular to the plate.

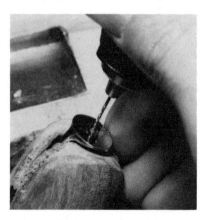

Fig. 3-3. Shows the center point being drilled.

Fig. 3-4. Use a bud bur to taper bore the hole.

STEP 4 — TAPER BORE THE HOLE
(Fig. 3-4)

Use a bud bur to taper bore the hole to a diameter just short that of the diamond being set. Continually check to see that the bore does not shift off center while it is being cut.

STEP 5 — CUT THE BEARING
(Fig. 3-5)

Cut the bearing with a high speed setting bur that is the same size as the diameter of the diamond being set. The depth of the bearing, in this case of a small diamond being set, should be at a level where the table of the diamond will set flush to the surface of the plate.

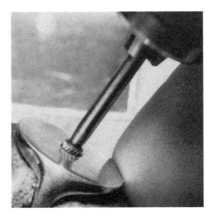

Fig. 3-5. Use a high speed setting bur to cut the bearing.

OPTION: ENGRAVE STAR EFFECTS
(Fig. 3-6)

This phase of star setting is related to STEP 8 — ENGRAVE EXCESS METAL, but is easier at this time before the diamond is seated and secured. The cuts are initially made at mid-distance between the locations where beads will be raised. For instance, if the beads will be raised along the center lines, then the cuts will be made between them or vice versa.

Use an onglette graver to cut the lines beginning about two millimeters from the bearing. The cuts should be made straight from the surface of the plate down through the vertex of the bearing toward the center of the hole. Afterwards each side of the cuts are bright cut toward the bearing (see fig. 3-7). The engravings should then appear as star points.

This is also an opportune time to remove abrasions from the surface of the plate. If the plate is scratched, use an emery stick with No. 3 emery paper to smooth the metal. Follow up with No. 4/0 polishing paper. The plate may also be pre-polished at this time. Once the diamond is seated and secured by raising beads, it will be difficult to keep the metal planed if scratches must be removed.

Fig. 3-6. Engrave star effects before seating the diamond.

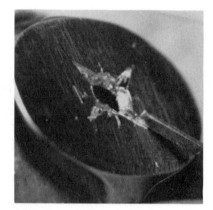

Fig. 3-7. Bright cut the star cuts.

STEP 6 — SEAT THE DIAMOND
(Fig. 3-8, 3-9, 3-10, 3-11)

The first phase of seating the diamond is to clean the bearing. To do this, lightly twist the setting bur into the bearing just enough to remove metal burrs that developed from the engraving and cutting the bearing. Metal burrs that extend above the surface from the bearing of a star setting should be removed with a flat graver (see fig. 3-8). In other types of settings a file is used to do this. Remaining debris can be removed by brushing. Also be sure that the diamond is clean.

Place the diamond into the bearing. Use bees wax to handle the diamond, but touch only the table area. Ideally the diamond should have to be slightly pressured into the bearing. A small piece of wood such as the edge of a ring clamp wedge will work fine. If it is difficult to slip the diamond into the bearing, do not force it. The bearing might need to be cut larger.

Fig. 3-8. Shows metal burrs that protrude from the rim of the bearing being removed by a flat graver.

Fig. 3-9. Brush debris from the bearing.

Fig. 3-10. Shows bees wax being used to place the diamond into the bearing.

Fig. 3-11. Shows a piece of wood being used to press the diamond into the bearing.

STEP 7 — SECURE THE DIAMOND
(Fig. 3-12, 3-13)

Depending upon the size of beads wanted, begin raising the beads from one half to one millimeter from the bearing. Push the tip of the round graver toward a point near the vertex of the bearing. The beads should be located between the star cuts. First raise all of the beads partially from opposite sides to be assured that the diamond will remain straight. Then go back and tighten the diamond by raising the beads up and onto the diamond. This is done by tilting the round graver to a higher angle.

Fig. 3-12. Shows the distance that a round graver is placed to begin raising a bead.

Fig. 3-13. Use a round graver to raise the beads.

STEP 8 — ENGRAVE EXCESS METAL
(Fig. 3-14)

The metal along each side of the beads is engraved to a point behind the bead. Begin by chasing the metal that was cut by the round graver to the base of the beads. Use an onglette graver. Then make fine straight cuts along each side of the beads from the bearing to the base behind each bead. Remove only enough metal to expose the beads.

STEP 9 — SHAPE THE BEADS
(Fig. 3-15)

Use a beading tool that has a compatible size tip to "round off" the beads. Keep the tool tilted away from the diamond so that only the raised burrs of metal are rounded.

Fig. 3-14. Use an onglette graver to remove the metal alongside the beads.

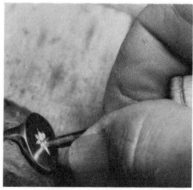

Fig. 3-15. Shows a beading tool being used to round off the beads.

STEP 10 — BRIGHT CUT THE METAL
(Fig. 3-16)

A flat graver having a polished tip is used to bright cut the metal that was cut along side each bead. Be careful that too much metal is not removed thereby distorting the intended design. Cut from the inside of the bearing straight toward the crevice of the star point behind each bead. Afterwards use the onglette graver again to chase the fine cuts behind the beads from the surface of the metal to the base of each bead.

Fig. 3-16. Bright cut the metal bordering the diamonds.

Fig. 3-17. A star set diamond.

2

Square Plate

The square is a basic design typically presented in jewelry. Square plates are used for bead setting solitaire diamonds, melee, and clusters. They are not confined to any particular fashion, but are more often applied to larger center diamonds such as that of a gents mounting. One popular advantage of this application is the possibility of a bright cut to border the diamond. A proficient bright cut in this case is necessary to heighten the illumination of the diamond thereby presenting the illusion of it being a larger diamond. An additional objective of bright cutting is to improve the attractiveness of the mounting. Setting a single diamond into a square plate is probably the most basic bead setting task to be learned by a diamond setter. This segment describes and illustrates that procedure. Bead setting a cluster of diamonds into a square plate is illustrated in Section IV.

STEP 1 — INSPECT THE MOUNTING
(Fig. 3-18)

Checklist:

(a) The true thickness of the plate on a mounting of this type cannot be visually checked. A millimeter gauge should be used to test the plate for thickness.

Fig. 3-18. Gents ring with a square center plate.

(b) Check to see that when the diamond is set lower into the plate it will not stick into the finger area.

(c) Inspect the mounting for weak areas. A single large center diamond will be set into this ring that requires extra large beads. The mounting must be able to withstand the pressure that is necessary to raise the beads.

(d) Place the diamond table down on the plate to be assured that there is plenty of space for the diamond to be set.

Fig. 3-19. Use dividers to engrave a circle centered on the plate that is the diameter of the diamond being set.

STEP 2 — DESIGN THE LAYOUT
(Fig. 3-19)

The center of a square plate is found by engraving diagonal lines across the plate from opposite corners. It will help for later reference to also engrave a circle on the plate from the center point with dividers. The circle, being the diameter of the diamond, will serve as a border for all drilling, taper boring, and bearing cutting. With this the diamond will be set centered into the plate.

STEP 3 — DRILL THE HOLE
(Fig. 3-20)

Some plates such as the one in the photographs are often very thick and require extensive drilling. Keep the drill cool by continually dipping it into cooling fluid. Also use a moderate drill speed to avoid breaking the drill.

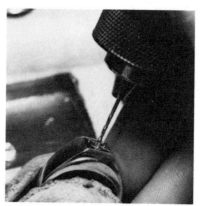

Fig. 3-20. Shows a hole being drilled
through the center point of the
plate.

STEP 4 — TAPER BORE THE HOLE
(Fig. 3-21, 3-22, 3-23, 3-24)

Since a large taper bore is necessary in this case, two sizes of bud burs are used. The first one being smaller is used to excavate the hole for the larger bore. In this manner the larger bud bur will not be subjected to excessive strain. By using only the larger bur, the mounting might become overheated and the bud bur could burn. The alternative is to select a larger drill to drill the hole.

Fig. 3-21. Begin a large taper bore with
a smaller bud bur.

Fig. 3-22. Taper boring a large hole.

Fig. 3-23. Shows a completed taper bore.

Fig. 3-24. The diameter of a taper bore should be a little shorter than the diameter of the diamond.

STEP 5 — CUT THE BEARING
(Fig. 3-25)

When bead setting a large diamond it is particularly important that the correct size bearing is gradually cut because there is a lot of metal to be removed. Beginning with the same size setting bur as the diamond, usually results in a larger bearing than expected (see CUT THE BEARING, pg. 60). The recommendation is to cut a smaller bearing, then follow-up with the correct size high speed setting bur. In essence, the bur will make a finer bearing if less metal has to be cut because there will be less pressure exerted to it.

Fig. 3-25. Use a high speed setting bur to cut the bearing.

Fig. 3-26. Using a barrette needle file to remove metal burrs that extend from the rim of the bearing.

STEP 6 — SEAT THE DIAMOND

(Fig. 3-26, 3-27)

Use a file to remove metal burrs that protrude above the plate from the newly cut bearing. Next, brush the plate and bearing to remove filings, shavings, and other debris. Then clean the diamond. The diamond can be pushed into the bearing by a fingernail, as shown in fig. 3-27, or another method described in Section II — SEAT THE DIAMOND.

STEP 7 — SECURE THE DIAMOND

(Fig. 3-28)

Use a No. 53 round graver to raise the beads onto the diamond from the corners of the plate. To keep the beads square to the diamond, engrave a faint line from each corner of the plate directly toward the center of the plate. This can be done with an onglette graver or scriber. Follow the engraved lines while raising the beads.

Fig. 3-27. Shows a finger nail being used to adjust the level of a diamond in a bearing before securing it.

Fig. 3-28. Shows a round graver being used to raise beads onto a diamond from the corners of the plate.

STEP 8 — ENGRAVE EXCESS METAL

(Fig. 3-29, 3-30)

Begin removing excess metal by first carving a straight line from the corners of the plate down to the base of the bead in those corners. Do this with an onglette graver. The cuts define the square and act as boundaries for the lengthy border cuts. Having a crevice carved in the corners makes it easier to control the graver and avoid cutting through the edge of the plate when other metal is engraved. Border metal is engraved straight between the bases of corner beads, along the girdle of the diamond, and beveled to the edge of the plate.

Fig. 3-29. Begin engraving excess metal by cutting from the corners of the plate to the base of the beads with an onglette graver.

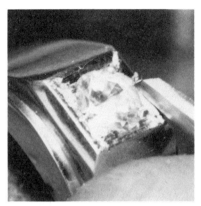

Fig. 3-30. Shows an onglette graver held at a slant to bevel the metal from the girdle of the diamond to the edge of the plate.

STEP 9 — SHAPE THE BEADS
(Fig. 3-31)

The metal burrs (beads) raised to secure the diamond are rounded by a beading tool. After the beads are formed, flattened metal usually develops around the beads and extends onto the diamond. This clinging metal can be removed by shaving it with a sharp flat graver.

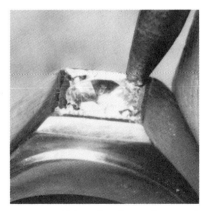

Fig. 3-31. Using a beading tool to round off the beads.

Fig. 3-32. Bright cut the engraved metal.

STEP 10 — BRIGHT CUT THE METAL
(Fig. 3-32, 3-33, 3-34, 3-35)

The bright cut should smooth the engraved metal to a mirror finish. A flat graver having a polished tip is used to do this. First use short shaving strokes until the length of each border can be bright cut by one continuous stroke. The flat graver will occasionally have to be sharpened and its tip polished.

The edge of the plate might be ragged or uneven after bright cutting. Trim the metal with a flat hand file by beveling the sides of the plate to the bright cuts. An emery stick should be used after filing to remove the file marks. Afterwards, if desired, the edge can be milligrained.

Fig. 3-33. Shows a flat hand file being used to trim the edge of the plate.

Fig. 3-34. Shows an emery stick being used to remove file marks from the edge of the plate.

Fig. 3-35. Shows a milligrain tool being used on the edge of the plate.

Fig. 3-36. Shows a diamond bead set into a square plate.

3

Triangle Plate

Triangle plates are commonly used on jewelry for setting melee, although it is not a rarity to see them used as center settings. One frequently applied design consists of two triangle plates soldered in line with a square center plate between them. The triangle plates, one on each side, are either butted against the center plate or slightly separated, and taper away from the center. Triangle plates are also used for earrings, pendants, and center diamonds on rings. In either case, the primary feature is the simplicity of the design. It is a change from the usual in that it offers a certain degree of geometric shape other than the round or square. Bead setting a diamond into a triangle plate is similar to the order of events to setting a square plate. The obvious difference is that there are only three sides with which to contend. This segment illustrates bead setting a single diamond into a triangle plate. To introduce a variation, two beads are raised at each point rather than one.

STEP 1 — INSPECT THE MOUNTING
(Fig. 3-37)

Checklist:

(a) Check the thickness of the triangle plate with a millimeter degree gauge. Determine if the bearing can be cut to an adequate depth.

(b) Be sure that when the diamond is set into the plate its culet will not protrude into the finger space.

(c) Inspect the undergallery that supports the plate, and ring shank, for strength requirements.

(d) Compare the diameter of the diamond to the size of the plate. The diamond should not extend over the edge of the plate.

STEP 2 — DESIGN A LAYOUT
(Fig. 3-38)

The center of the triangle (if it is an equilateral triangle) can be found by engraving lines from each vertex to a point that bisects its opposite side.

107

In fig. 3-38 dividers are shown engraving a circle from the center point. The circle is made equal to the diameter of the diamond or a bit smaller. All taper boring and bearing cutting is maintained within the circle to be assured that the diamond will be set centered in the plate.

Fig. 3-37. Shows a ring with a triangle center plate.

Fig. 3-38. Use dividers to lay out the plate.

STEP 3 — DRILL THE HOLE

(Fig. 3-39)

Drill a hole through the center of the plate. To avoid drilling off center, or slipping, a starter hole is made for the drill. A round graver is used to do this by picking an indentation into the metal at the center point.

Fig. 3-39. Shows a hole being drilled into the center of a triangle plate.

Fig. 3-40. Use a bud bur to taper bore the hole.

STEP 4 — TAPER BORE THE HOLE
(Fig. 3-40)

A taper bore will alleviate much of the work prior to cutting the bearing. Use a bud bur that has a diameter just short that of the diamond being set. Excavate the metal with the bud bur until the bur is submerged about halfway into the metal. Continually check while boring to make sure that it is kept centered within the engraved circle.

STEP 5 — CUT THE BEARING
(Fig. 3-41)

Use a high speed setting bur to cut the bearing. Tests might have to be made by placing the diamond in and out of the bearing to determine the correct depth. The depth of the bearing depends on the size of the diamond being set (see fig. 2-19, pg. 62).

Fig. 3-41. Use a high speed setting bur to cut the bearing.

Fig. 3-42. Shows a rim of metal burrs that form while a bearing is being cut.

STEP 6 — SEAT THE DIAMOND
(Fig. 3-42, 3-43, 3-44)

Figure 3-42 shows a rim of metal burrs that commonly extend above the plate after a bearing is cut. This metal should be removed by lightly filing before seating the diamond in order to estimate the actual depth of the bearing. The bearing is then brushed clean. The diamond is also cleaned by tumbling it over a bench cloth or between a thumb and finger.

Push the diamond into the bearing. Figure 3-43 shows a metal rod extending from the bees wax tool being used to push the diamond into the bearing. Then a fingernail is shown pressing on the diamond to make a final adjustment to level it.

Fig. 3-43. Shows a metal rod being used to push the diamond into the bearing.

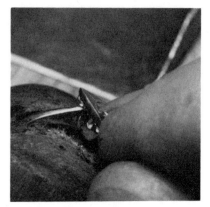

Fig. 3-44. Shows a fingernail being used to adjust the diamond in the bearing.

STEP 7 — SECURE THE DIAMOND
(Fig. 3-45)

Two beads are raised onto the diamond at each corner (this is an option). They are placed adjacent to the previously engraved lines that extend from the corners. This is done to maintain equal spacing among the pairs of beads. Begin by raising one bead at each corner until the diamond is secure enough that it will not tilt out of level, then raise the adjacent beads.

Fig. 3-45. Shows a round graver being used to raise two beads at each corner.

Fig. 3-46. Use an onglette graver to remove metal between the beads.

STEP 8 — ENGRAVE EXCESS METAL
(Fig. 3-46)

First the three borders are carved at a bevel from the diamond to the edge of the plate. Use an onglette graver. These should be straight cuts. Do not curve the metal around the contour of the diamond. Then the metal between the pairs of beads is split at a bevel from the diamond to the base of the border.

STEP 9 — SHAPE THE BEADS
(Fig. 3-47)

Use a beading tool to form the beads. All beads should become equal in size and shape. Further trimming of the beads can be done with a sharp flat graver or by chasing previously engraved metal adjacent to the beads with the onglette graver.

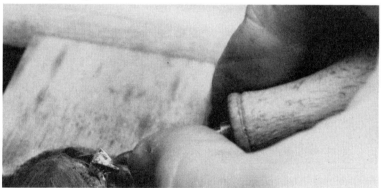

Fig. 3-47. Use a beading tool to form the beads.

STEP 10 — BRIGHT CUT THE METAL
(Fig. 3-48, 3-49, 3-50, 3-51, 3-52)

Bright cut the metal between the pairs of beads first. Use a flat graver that has a polished tip. Next bright cut the three borders. The inside metal is finished first because the bordering metal, if it has previously been brightened, will be distorted by the flat graver.

Trim the outside edge of the plate to the bright cut with a flat hand file or barrette needle file. The resulting file marks could be removed with emery paper, but in figure 3-51 a large rubber wheel is shown being used to do the same. If a rubber wheel is used, the edge of it should be flattened first. This is done by rotating it against a flat hand file (see fig. 3-50). A milligrain is then applied to decorate the edge of the plate if it is requested.

Fig. 3-48. Use a flat graver to bright cut the engraved metal.

Fig. 3-49. Shows a flat hand file being used to trim the edges of the plate.

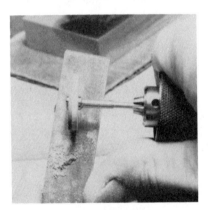

Fig. 3-50. Shows a large rubber wheel being flattened on the edge by rotating it against a flat hand file.

Fig. 3-51. Using a large rubber wheel to remove file marks on the edges of the plate.

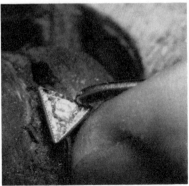

Fig. 3-52. Shows a milligrain being applied.

Fig. 3-53. Shows a diamond bead set into a triangle plate.

4

Hexagon Plate

Hexagon plates, those having six equal sides and angles, are further adaptations of the square and triangle. They are primarily standard in antique designs that are outlined by filigree and other delicate designs. Although these ornamental fashions are somewhat limited in today's marketplace, they are occasionally found. An interesting provision of bead setting a diamond into a hexagon plate is the detail of the work involved. A series of six equally spaced beads are raised to secure the diamond; some beads may serve merely for decorative purposes. Also, engraving and bright cutting the surrounding metal to form six equal facets of metal becomes quite challenging. When bead setting a diamond into a hexagon plate, special emphasis is given to the repetition of events in order to symmetrically form the border. This is a likeliness of the square and triangle plate that were previously discussed, but it is an expanded version.

STEP 1 — INSPECT THE MOUNTING

(Fig. 3-54)

Checklist:

(a) A filigree mounting, such as the one in the photograph, could involve many problems. One problem has to do with the true thickness of the plate. Measure the plate with a millimeter degree gauge to see if an adequate bearing can be cut.

(b) Next, be sure that the culet of the diamond will not extend too far into the finger area. Since there is so much vacant space under the filigree, the wearer's finger will fill some of that space.

(c) The mounting shown in the photographs obviously has less strength because of the filigree. It will have to be packed with diamond setters cement. This will be done later after the bulk of machining has been completed. Otherwise heat developed during the machining will melt the cement causing it to flow into the setting area. The cutting burs will then become dull because diamond setters cement is also an abrasive.

(d) One final check is to determine if the plate is wide enough to accept the diameter of the diamond.

STEP 2 — DESIGN A LAYOUT

(Fig. 3-55)

Engrave lines on the plate between opposite corners. The intersection will be the center. If the diamond being set is fairly large, a circle may be engraved from the center point to control the limits of taper boring and bearing cutting.

Fig. 3-54. Shows a filigree ring with a hexagon plate.

Fig. 3-55. Shows lines engraved between opposite corners, and dividers engraving a circle that represents the diameter of the diamond to be set.

STEP 3 — DRILL THE HOLE

Use moderate pressure when drilling, especially in this type of mounting. If the drill is not controlled while it completes the hole, it could thrust into the filigree undergallery and distort the design.

STEP 4 — TAPER BORE THE HOLE

(Fig. 3-56)

Use a bud bur to taper bore the hole. Apply as little pressure as necessary to bore the hole because some filigree mountings will collapse easily. Do not bore the hole beyond the diameter of the diamond. It is best to be safe and keep the diameter of the bore smaller than the diamond. However, it should be large enough to help the setting bur cut an accurate bearing.

STEP 5 — CUT THE BEARING
(Fig. 3-57)

Cut the bearing with a high speed setting bur to the appropriate depth and diameter of the diamond. Cooling fluid will help the bur to cut the metal. Also the pressure applied to the plate will have to be restricted.

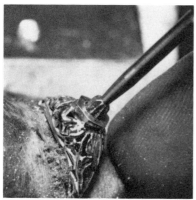

Fig. 3-56. Shows the maximum depth that a bud bur is inserted to taper bore the hole.

Fig. 3-57. Shows a high speed setting bur being used to cut the bearing.

STEP 6 — SEAT THE DIAMOND
(Fig. 3-58, 3-59, 3-60, 3-61)

Before seating the diamond, the mounting is packed with diamond setters cement. This is done by melting some cement on the cement stick until

Fig. 3-58. Shows a small amount of warmed diamond setters cement being pulled from a cement stick to reinforce the fragile filigree.

Fig. 3-59. Shows diamond setters cement protruding into the bearing and filigree after packing.

a sufficient amount which can be packed under the filigree undergallery becomes pliable like putty. When the cement becomes cool enough to handle but still warm, the necessary amount can be pulled from the stick (see fig. 3-58). Quickly fill the vacant area under the plate until the cement begins to protrude through the filigree, then secure the ring into the ring clamp. After the cement cools it will be hard. A small worn bud bur, or drill, can be used to remove the cement that hardens in the bearing. Remember that the cement will dull a sharp bur. Brush the setting clear of remaining debris and clean the diamond. Lastly, place the diamond into the bearing.

Fig. 3-60. Use a worn bud bur to remove diamond setters cement from the bearing.

Fig. 3-61. Brush loose debris from the bearing.

STEP 7 — SECURE THE DIAMOND

(Fig. 3-62)

Partially raise a bead from each corner of the plate toward the diamond until the diamond is fairly snug. When the diamond can no longer shift, return to each bead and tighten them onto the diamond. Always work from opposite sides of a diamond when raising beads.

STEP 8 — ENGRAVE EXCESS METAL

(Fig. 3-63)

Using an onglette graver first cut from the edge of the plate at each corner down to the base of each bead. This defines the corners by chasing over the cuts previously made by the round graver. Afterwards carve the six sides that border the diamond. Engrave a straight path from the bases of the beads along the girdle of the diamond and beveled to the edge of the plate. The onglette graver will have to be held at a slant to do this.

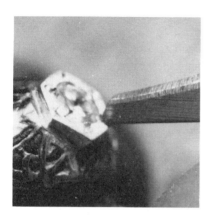

Fig. 3-62. Shows a round graver being used to raise beads onto the diamond.

Fig. 3-63. Use an onglette graver to bevel the metal from corner to corner along the girdle of the diamond.

STEP 9 — SHAPE THE BEADS

(Fig. 3-64)

Use a beading tool that has a compatible size tip to round off the beads. To do this the beading tool is rotated in a circular path while simultaneously twisting on the bead.

Fig. 3-65. Shows a flat graver being used to bright cut the metal.

Fig. 3-64. Using a beading tool to round off the beads.

STEP 10 — BRIGHT CUT THE METAL

(Fig. 3-65, 3-66, 3-67)

The six bordering sides are bright cut with a flat graver that has a polished tip. The finish of each border should become planed and smooth. Afterwards use a barrette needle file to trim the edge of the plate to the bright cuts. Later the edge can be milligrained if desired.

Fig. 3-66. Shows a barrette needle file being used to trim the edges of the plate.

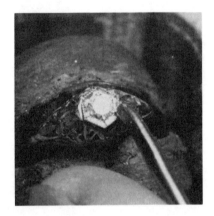

Fig. 3-67. Milligrain the edges of the plate.

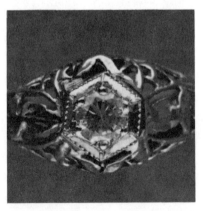

Fig. 3-68. Shows a diamond bead set into a hexagon plate.

5

Marquis Plate

Marquis shaped plates are typically found on mountings that require bead setting. A common example that is illustrated in this application is to set two small diamonds close together into the plate. If the diamonds are set girdle-to-girdle, and the metal is engraved as specified, they can resemble a single marquis diamond. This arrangement may be duplicated to have multiple similar settings about a cluster or dinner ring that also employs other types of settings. The intentional effect is for the pairs of diamonds to appear as marquis cut melee supporting a larger configuration of diamonds or other center setting. There are common occurrences when the marquis plate is used by itself as a center setting. In those designs the area of metal might be capable of containing several diamonds. Bead setting two diamonds to resemble a single marquis diamond is discussed at this time since the procedure is so closely related to the previous application of triangle plates.

STEP 1 — INSPECT THE MOUNTING

(Fig. 3-69)

Checklist:

(a) A visual inspection of the mounting in figure 3-69 will determine if the plate is thick enough to accept the diamonds. Two smaller diamonds will be set so the depth of the bearings will not have to be cut too deep.

Fig. 3-69. Shows a ring with a marquis plate.

Fig. 3-70. Adjust the dividers from each end of the plate by trial and error to find the center point.

119

(b) The culets of the diamonds will not extend into the finger space of this particular ring because the plate is raised high above the mounting.

(c) The strength of the mounting should be considered when tightening the ring into the ring clamp. From its appearance the cut out designs in the ring might not withstand too much pressure. Also check under the plate to see how it is secured to the ring.

(d) To see if the surface of the plate is large enough to accept the two diamonds, place them tables down and girdle-to-girdle on the plate. There should be plenty of space for raising beads and bright cutting later.

STEP 2 — DESIGN A LAYOUT
(Fig. 3-70)

Engrave a straight dim line on the plate between the two points to find the center line. From each end of the line adjust the dividers by trial and error as shown in figure 3-70 to find the center point. The center point will be equal distance from each end. Next place the diamonds on the center line of the plate and adjacent to its center point to project and mark the center points of the diamonds. Then remove the diamonds and engrave the center points of the diamonds.

STEP 3 — DRILL THE HOLES
(Fig. 3-71)

Drill a hole through the two center points of the diamonds. Dip the drill into cooling fluid often to keep the drill cool and to help it to cut into the metal.

Fig. 3-71. Shows a hole being drilled at each of the two center points for the two diamonds.

Fig. 3-72. Use a bud bur to taper bore the holes.

STEP 4 — TAPER BORE THE HOLES
(Fig. 3-72)

Taper bore the holes with a bud bur using the center point and center line of the plate as a guideline. The diamonds should be set girdle-to-girdle, but the bores are to be a little smaller than the diameters of the diamonds. Because of the smaller holes, there should be a little space left untouched at the center of the plate. Later, when the bearings are cut to the same size as the diameter of the diamonds, they may be tangent at the center of the plate.

STEP 5 — CUT THE BEARINGS
(Fig. 3-73)

Use a high speed setting bur to cut the bearings. Do not assume that the two diamonds are exactly the same size. The size of the girdles and diameters of each diamond could vary. Several tool changes might have to be made in order to select the correct size bur for each diamond.

Fig. 3-73. Use a high speed setting bur to cut the bearings.

Fig. 3-74. Shows a barrette needle file being used to remove metal burrs that extend from the newly cut bearings.

STEP 6 — SEAT THE DIAMONDS
(Fig. 3-74, 3-75)

Clean the bearings by first using a barrette needle file to remove the protrusions of metal burrs that developed when the bearings were cut. Then twist the setting bur into each bearing once more to remove filings, shavings, and other debris. Afterwards clean the diamonds and place them into the appropriate bearings.

Fig. 3-75. Use a brush to remove loose
debris from the bearings.

STEP 7 — SECURE THE DIAMONDS
(Fig. 3-76)

Three beads are raised onto each diamond by a round graver. The bead at each point is obviously placed along the center line of the plate, but the center beads require a little more judgment. Those beads should be started from a perspective or actual engraved border that extends from alongside the girdles of the diamonds. This curved line follows the contour of the plate and will become the location of the bright cut that borders the diamonds later. Begin each bead on the line just far enough from the diamond to raise a sufficient amount of metal to secure it. Raising beads in this manner will ensure that they will be symmetrically spaced.

Fig. 3-76. Use a round graver to raise
the beads.

STEP 8 — ENGRAVE EXCESS METAL

(Fig. 3-77)

The excess metal is engraved to expose the beads and diamonds. Use an onglette graver. First cut from the points of the plate to the bases of the beads there. Next, trim the metal on each side of the plate along the girdles of the diamonds. These cuts should curve from corner to corner, and bevel to the edge of the plate. Then carve the metal from the center beads to the base of the border cuts. Be careful not to engrave through the edge of the plate.

STEP 9 — SHAPE THE BEADS

(Fig. 3-78)

Round off the beads with a beading tool that has an adequate size concave tip. The beads at the points of the plate have a tendency to become larger because there was more space to raise the beads at those locations. This will not hamper the design if both beads are the same size.

Fig. 3-77. Use an onglette graver to remove excess metal.

Fig. 3-78. Shows a beading tool being used to shape the beads.

STEP 10 — BRIGHT CUT THE METAL
(Fig. 3-79, 3-80, 3-81)

Use a flat graver that has a polished tip to bright cut the engraved metal. Begin with the center engravings to avoid distorting the final contour cuts. Always chase over crevice cuts at points or corners with an onglette graver after bright cutting; it leaves a distinguished design on the plate. Upon completion use a barrette needle file to trim the edge of the plate. Then use a large rubber wheel to remove the file marks.

Fig. 3-79. Shows a flat graver being used to bright cut the metal.

Fig. 3-80. Shows a barrette needle file being used to trim the outside edge of the plate.

Fig. 3-81. Shows a large rubber wheel being used to smooth the outside edge of the plate.

Fig. 3-82. Shows two diamonds bead set into a marquis plate.

6

Bead Setting Diamonds Into A Row

Bead setting diamonds into a row or in-line is an application that is applied for the most part to wedding bands. There are numerous other mountings where diamonds are set in line, as a fraction of the design, that cannot be totally excluded here. However, for practical purposes, this segment will eliminate the unrelated sections of those elaborate mountings and confine the illustrations to the specific topic of discussion. Actually the task at hand is an extension of the procedure to bead set a diamond into a square plate. Instead of one diamond being set, a series of diamonds are identically set adjacent to each other and in line.

The manner that the surrounding metal is engraved and the closeness of the diamonds will determine the design. The bar of metal may be engraved into separate square sections, extended bright cuts could be made along both sides of the diamonds, or the metal may be engraved to present other unique effects. There are unlimited numbers of designs that can be engraved on a bar of metal containing a row of bead set diamonds. The most common of these are illustrated in this segment. Other designs based on those designs can be developed by the diamond setter as experience is obtained and the need for them arises.

STEP 1 — INSPECT THE MOUNTING
(Fig. 3-83)

Checklist:

(a) Determine if the plate metal is thick enough for the bearings to be cut. Figure 3-83 shows a plate soldered onto a solid band. There is usually enough depth in this type of mounting to cut the bearings.

(b) One common problem with a mounting such as the one being discussed is the possibility of the diamonds sticking through the band into the finger area. Check for this before beginning the work. Be careful later not to cut the bearings too deep even though the plate metal is thick.

(c) The mounting is noticeably strong enough to support the pressure required to machine and engrave it.

(d) Since a number of diamonds are to be set, they should all be temporarily placed on the plate to be sure that there is enough room for all of them to be set.

Fig. 3-83. Shows a ring with a bar of metal soldered onto it for bead setting a row of diamonds.

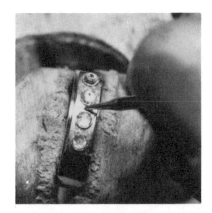

Fig. 3-84. Shows a scriber being used to engrave layout lines.

STEP 2 — DESIGN A LAYOUT

(Fig. 3-84, 3-85)

The diamonds are laid out on the plate to equally space them and mark the center points where they will be set. To do this first warm the plate just enough to smear a thin film of bees wax on it. Next, place the diamonds tables down on the plate and adjust the diamonds to the exact locations where they should be set. Use a graver or scriber to make tick marks between and along the side of each diamond. Then remove the diamonds to engrave other boundaries on the plate.

A border should be made with dividers as shown in figure 3-85 to keep the boring and bearing cutting in a straight line. The center points of the diamond and borders should be clearly marked in order to set the diamonds equally spaced and in a straight path.

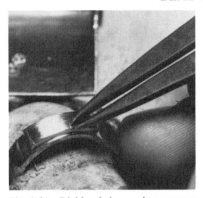

Fig. 3-85. Dividers being used to engrave straight borders.

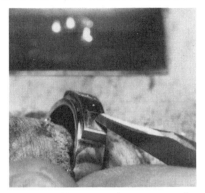

Fig. 3-86. Use a round graver to make indentations into the center points to start the drill holes.

STEP 3 — DRILL THE HOLES
(Fig. 3-86, 3-87)

Use a round graver to make a depression into each center point to start the drill holes. Drill each hole perpendicular to the contour of the plate at its location. When completed, the bottom of the holes under the plate should also be centered and equally spaced.

Fig. 3-87. Drill each hole perpendicular to its location on the plate.

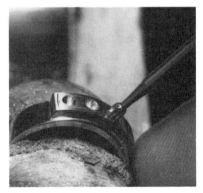

Fig. 3-88. Use a bud bur to taper bore the holes.

STEP 4 — TAPER BORE THE HOLES
(Fig. 3-88)

Use a bud bur to taper bore the holes. Continually check the spacing of the bores and keep them within the borders. The diameter of the bores should not be wider than the diameter of the diamonds, and the bores should taper from the surface of the plate (see fig. 2-17, pg. 57).

STEP 5 — CUT THE BEARINGS

(Fig. 3-89)

Use a high speed setting bur to cut the bearings. First cut the bearings with a bur that is slightly smaller than the diamonds, then work up to the correct size bur. This process will ensure that the bearings are not cut too wide. When completed, the high speed setting bur, as shown in figure 3-90, is used to counter bore the holes under the plate. This will remove metal burrs from the drilled holes and smooth the finger area of the ring.

Fig. 3-89. Use a high speed setting bur to cut the bearings.

Fig. 3-90. Shows a high speed setting bur being used to counter bore the holes under the plate.

STEP 6 — SEAT THE DIAMONDS

(Fig. 3-91, 3-92)

Brush the bearings clear of debris and clean the diamonds before seating them into the bearings. Figure 3-91 shows a diamond being pushed into a bearing by pressing on its table facet with the edge of a wood wedge. Figure 3-92 shows the ring being shaded from the bench light by holding one hand a couple inches above the plate. By doing this the level of the diamonds can be seen better.

Fig. 3-91. Shows a piece of wood being used to press the diamonds into the bearings.

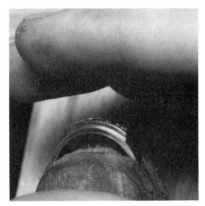

Fig. 3-92. Shade the seated diamonds from the bench light to observe if they are all seated level.

STEP 7 — SECURE THE DIAMONDS

(Fig. 3-93)

Use a round graver to raise four (optional) beads onto each diamond. The beads of each diamond should be squared around it. Also, the beads of all diamonds should be in line across the plate. To keep the beads in line begin all of them from the previously engraved edge borders just far enough from the diamonds to get a good size bead onto the diamonds.

Fig. 3-93. Use a round graver to raise the beads.

Fig. 3-94. Begin engraving excess metal by first carving the corners of the plate to the bases of the corner beads.

STEP 8 — ENGRAVE EXCESS METAL
(Fig. 3-94, 3-95)

The excess metal is engraved with an onglette graver to emboss the diamonds and beads from the plate. First cut the corners from the edge of the plate down the bases of the corner beads (see fig. 3-94). These crevices will help to outline the design and keep the border carvings that will be made later from slipping through the edge of the plate. The four borders are carved from corner-to-corner along the bases of the beads and girdles of the diamonds. All of these cuts should be straight and beveled to the edge of the plate.

In the accompanying series of photographs the option of a star cut is engraved between the diamonds. This is done by making four short and straight cuts between the adjacent diamonds. Each of the carvings are begun near the center of the plate from the girdles of the diamonds. Make the cuts beveled to a point between the two beads that secure adjacent diamonds.

Fig. 3-95. Use an onglette graver to bevel the metal from the girdles of the diamonds to the edge of the plate.

Fig. 3-96. Use a beading tool to shape the beads.

STEP 9 — SHAPE THE BEADS

(Fig. 3-96)

The beads should all be rounded to a uniform size. The beading tool might have to be re-shaped a few times before the phase is completed. Occasionally some beads are difficult to shape. This problem is often solved by cutting more adjacent metal away from those beads to further expose the beads. Use a flat graver to trim flattened metal that forms from the beads onto the diamonds.

Fig. 3-98. Using a flat graver to bright cut the metal that borders the diamonds.

Fig. 3-97. Shows the metal between the beads being bright cut.

STEP 10 — BRIGHT CUT THE METAL

(Fig. 3-97, 3-98, 3-99, 3-100)

Use a flat graver that has a polished tip to bright cut the metal between the diamonds and along the four borders. Bright cut the metal between the diamonds first, then the borders. Alternative means to supplement the bright cuts at the borders are shown in figures 3-99 and 3-100. Respectively, a fine cutting three corner needle file and/or a knife edge pumice wheel can be used to a certain extent on the lengthy borders.

When the bright cutting is complete, use a flat hand file to trim the edge of the plate to the bright cuts. Afterwards, emery the file marks. The outside edge of the plate should be smoothed as much as feasible by the diamond setter to avoid excessive polishing later.

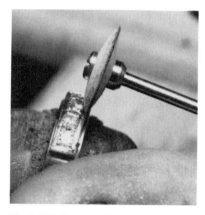

Fig. 3-99. Shows a fine cut-three corner needle file being used to smooth the border as an alternate to bright cutting.

Fig. 3-100. Shows a knife edge pumice wheel being used to smooth the border as an alternate to bright cutting.

Fig. 3-101. Shows a row of diamonds bead set with star cuts between the diamonds.

Fig. 3-102. Shows an example of diamonds secured by two beads.

7

Bead Setting Diamonds Into A Curve

Bead setting diamonds into circular paths or swirls is commonly applied to clusters - primarily dinner ring types that combine a number of geometric shapes. Other applications include ring guards and the upcoming cluster designs in the following section. The illustrations presented in this segment pertain to a basic curve of bead set diamonds. This is an advanced version of the previous segment that illustrates bead setting diamonds into rows. The fundamental procedure used for that application is expanded to bead setting diamonds into curvature designs. Some feature differences are the spacing of the beads and bright cuts. After the diamond setter becomes proficient enough to bead set diamonds into circular paths, the advanced section of pavé setting should be easily obtainable.

STEP 1 — INSPECT THE MOUNTING
(Fig. 3-103)

Checklist:

(a) The horse-shoe ring in the series of photographs is shown having three small diamonds set into the raised plate at the arc. The first inspection is to see if that plate is thick enough to machine. In this case the inspection can be performed visually without mechanical means.

(b) The plate is embossed from the ring, and the diamonds are small. There should be no problem with the culets of the diamonds sticking into the finger.

(c) The shank and undergallery of the ring appear to be strong enough to support the pressure required to bead set the diamonds.

(d) A test will have to be made to see if the diamonds will fit into the plate without having the girdles extend through the edge. To make the observation, place the diamonds on the plate.

STEP 2 — DESIGN A LAYOUT
(Fig. 3-104)

Designing a layout of diamonds into a curve can be deceiving at times.

133

The center points for any number of diamonds are easily misinterpreted. It is better to lay the diamonds out on the plate and mark their locations rather than assume where they will fit. A scriber, as shown in figure 3-104, or graver can be used to do this. Engrave light border marks between and around the diamonds. When the diamonds are removed, the centers can be marked with reasonable accuracy.

Fig. 3-103. Shows a horse-shoe ring having a curved plate at the arch.

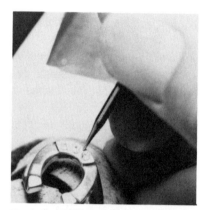

Fig. 3-104. Shows a scriber being used to engrave border marks between and around the diamonds.

STEP 3 — DRILL THE HOLES
(Fig. 3-105, 3-106)

Drill the holes at the center points. Keep the drill cool by occasionally dipping it into cooling fluid as shown in figure 3-105.

Fig. 3-105. Keep the drill cool by occasionally dipping it into cutting oil.

Fig. 3-106. Shows holes being drilled.

STEP 4 — TAPER BORE THE HOLES

(Fig. 3-107)

Use a bud bur to taper bore the holes to a diameter that is slightly less than that of the diamonds. The diamonds will be set close in this situation, so be extra careful to maintain equal spacing. If a bore begins to drift off center, it can be "pulled" during the early stages by tilting the bud bur as shown in figure 2-18, pg. 58.

Fig. 3-107. Use a bud bur to taper bore the holes.

Fig. 3-108. Use a high speed setting bur to cut the bearings.

STEP 5 — CUT THE BEARINGS

(Fig. 3-108)

Cut the center bearing first, then the adjacent bearings in case the other bearings have to be pulled farther away. After the center bearing is cut by a high speed setting bur, the seating of the diamonds and border size can be foreseen.

STEP 6 — SEAT THE DIAMONDS

(Fig. 3-109, 3-110)

File any metal burrs that might protrude from the bearing. After being sure that the bearings and diamonds are clean, the diamonds can be seated. The diamonds should fit snug and to a level where the table facets are flush to the surface of the plate. This will ensure good size beads and adequate bright cuts later.

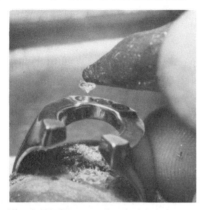

Fig. 3-109. Shows a diamond being handled via bees wax to place it into a bearing.

Fig. 3-110. Shows a diamond being seated into a bearing by pressing on it with a piece of wood.

STEP 7 — SECURE THE DIAMONDS
(Fig. 3-111)

A round graver is used to pry beads onto the diamonds. The beads at the shorter curve will be closer together than those at the expanded curve. One particular point of concern in this case is that since there is not much metal between the diamonds and the edge of the plate, raising the beads will be tricky. There is a tendency for the graver to slip back and down rather than toward the diamonds. This resistance can be compensated for by keeping the graver at a low angle until the beads begin to reach onto the diamonds.

Fig. 3-111. Shows a round graver prying a burr of metal (bead) onto a diamond to secure it.

Fig. 3-112. Use an onglette graver to engrave excess metal.

STEP 8 — ENGRAVE EXCESS METAL
(Fig. 3-112)

First cut the corners from the edge of the plate to the base of the beads there, then carve the bordering metal. The border metal is engraved behind the beads at each corner along the girdles of the diamonds and beveled to the edge of the plate. The onglette graver will have to be slanted in order to bevel the metal. In this situation the metal between the diamonds, and the beads there, can be removed by single straight cuts at girdle level from border-to-border across the plate.

STEP 9 — SHAPE THE BEADS
(Fig. 3-113)

A beading tool inserted into the handpiece of a flex-shaft machine and being used to shape the beads is shown in figure 3-113. A certain amount of additional engraving of excess metal might be necessary if the beads do not form correctly. When the flex-shaft machine is used rather than a beading tool handle, be sure that the concave tip of the beading tool revolves centered (see SHAPE THE BEADS, pg. 77).

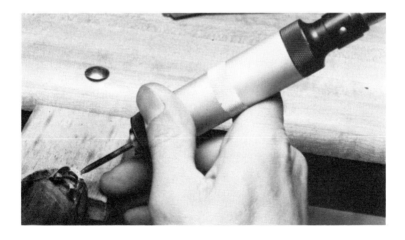

Fig. 3-113. Shows a beading tool being used with the flex-shaft machine to round off the beads.

STEP 10 — BRIGHT CUT THE METAL
(Fig. 3-114, 3-115, 3-116)

Since the diamonds are set very close together in this example, there is no metal between the diamonds to bright cut. Only the edge border can be bright cut. There will be some difficulty to bright cut the shorter curve because of the arched contour. One recommendation here is to smooth it as much as possible with the flat graver without removing too much metal. Then go over it with a knife edge pumice wheel. Later the sides of the plate are trimmed with a barrette and half round needle file.

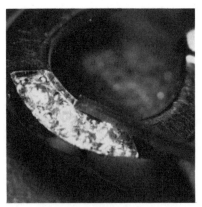

Fig. 3-114. Shows a flat graver being used to bright cut the engraved metal.

Fig. 115.   Shows a barrette needle file beng used to trim the outside edge of the plate.

Fig. 116.   Shows a half round needle file being used to trim the plate from inside the horse shoe.

Fig. 3-117. Shows a curve of bead set diamonds.

SECTION IV

Advanced Pavé Setting

Introduction

Pavé setting offers the most gratifying work for diamond setters. Probably no other task confronted in the craft is completed with so much of a sense of pride and personal esteem. Mental and physical capabilities of the highest caliber of craftsmanship are combined to assemble a configuration of diamonds into a blank plate of metal. Some diamond mountings display a single basic design, and others elaborately consist of several different figures of metal. Because of the dedicated craftsman's innate behavior, satisfaction will be found by seeking complexity over mere simplicity.

Individual opinions differ as to the exact meaning of pavé setting. The controversy among jewelry craftsmen seems to correlate with personal degrees of experience, expertise, and skill. For instance, a lesser experienced novice or layman may define pavé setting as simply bead or plate setting. A jeweler, designer, or bench worker having several years' experience in the jewelry industry might define pavé setting with a more expanded and detailed version.

The most basic form of pavé setting is to bead set a single diamond into a plate of metal. However, this is a simplification and not entirely definitive because a single diamond does not cover all of the metal. A more accurate definition is to set a number of diamonds close together into a plate of metal. Furthermore, the diamonds are to be tightly packed in a configuration that when excess metal is removed only the beads and diamonds are exposed from the plate. The diamonds should cover or pave the metal as if to conceal it.

This advanced section defines and illustrates pavé setting as it is known to experienced craftsmen. The format follows the previous section by first presenting common shapes of mountings and then progresses to mountings that employ finer details. Various shapes of clusters are illustrated in a sequence that gradually introduces more and more complexity. The procedures to set clusters of diamonds into square and round plates are first described. These are presented to familiarize the diamond setter with bead setting diamonds close together. Next, an oval and a pear shaped cluster are shown being pavé set. These clusters involve a higher echelon of diamond setting that both reviews and expands from the former procedures. They also include some unique deviations from the basic bead setting procedure. The geometrics increase with each cluster to show how a number of bead setting applications can blend together in an arrangement on a mounting. Lastly an elaborate mounting is introduced to illustrate the advanced procedure of pavé setting diamonds.

1

Square Cluster

A square cluster is shown in this segment being bead set to illustrate the formation of a pavé cluster. In the beginning of Section III a single diamond was bead set into a square plate. That assembly was said to be a basic bead setting procedure. Later in Section III a series of diamonds were bead set into a row to present an expanded version of that fundamental application. Now the procedure is even further advanced to demonstrate how a basic bead setting skill can be repeated on a larger mounting to form a pavé set cluster. The less experienced diamond setter is encouraged to refer to those basic procedures from time to time until each phase becomes second hand. This segment includes each phase of the bead setting procedure, but some of the more basic details that were discussed in Sections II and III might have to be reviewed.

STEP 1 — INSPECT THE MOUNTING

(Fig. 4-1)

Checklist:

(a) The plate shown in figure 4-1 is soldered onto the gents ring but might not be as thick as it appears. Use a millimeter degree gauge to measure it to be assured that the bearings can be cut to an adequate depth.

(b) Check to see that the plate is high enough that the culets of the diamonds will not extend to the finger of the wearer.

(c) Visually inspect the mounting for weak areas that could restrict the pressure that will be applied to the ring. The thickness of the plate is also a strength factor about which to be concerned. Since several diamonds are to be set, the plate will become even weaker because much of the metal will be removed in order to cut the bearings.

(d) Space the diamonds on the plate to determine if they will all fit. This should be a visual inspection.

145

Fig. 4-1.   Shows a gents ring with a large square plate.

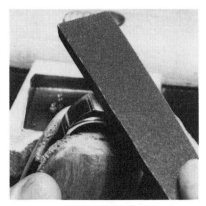

Fig. 4-2.   Emery the plate so that distinct layout marks can be seen.

STEP 2 — DESIGN A LAYOUT

(Fig. 4-2, 4-3, 4-4)

At this time decisions are made concerning the placement of beads, how the metal will be engraved later, and the expected width of the bordering bright cuts. First emery the plate so that distinct layout marks can be engraved (see fig. 4-2). Crossing center lines are determined by trial-and-error by adjusting the dividers from opposite sides of the plate. Then equally space three diamonds on one line and engrave tick marks alongside them (see fig. 4-3). These will denote other center lines.

There will be three rows of diamonds set. The center lines are scratched by one point of the dividers. Use the outside of the plate as a straight edge for the other point to slide (see fig. 4-4). When completed there should be nine center points clearly marked on the center lines.

Fig. 4-3.   Shows center lines being engraved with a scriber.

Fig. 4-4.   Using dividers to engrave straight center lines.

STEP 3 — DRILL THE HOLES
(Fig. 4-5, 4-6)

Use a round graver to make an indentation at each center point to serve as starter holes for the drill (see fig. 4-5). It is important that.the holes are all equally spaced. The indentations will help to keep the drill from slipping off center. Carefully drill all the holes. Occasionally dip the drill into cooling fluid to reduce friction and to help the drill to work.

Fig. 4-5.   Shows a round graver being used to indent center points.

Fig. 4-6.   Shows holes being drilled.

STEP 4 — TAPER BORE THE HOLES
(Fig. 4-7)

Taper bore the holes with a bud bur. They should be equally spaced and nearly the diameter of the diamonds. Begin by boring three holes across the center of the plate, then bore the adjacent holes. All rows of bored holes should be parallel when completed. While boring, try to anticipate problems that could arise later when the beads will be raised and the metal engraved.

Fig. 4-7. Using a bud bur to taper bore the holes.

Fig. 4-8. Shows a high speed setting bur cutting the bearings.

STEP 5 — CUT THE BEARINGS
(Fig. 4-8)

Use a high speed setting bur to cut the bearings. Some bearings will likely have to be cut to different levels and/or widths to accommodate various sizes of diamonds. Those bearings should be clearly marked and the particular diamonds separated. A considerable amount of time is usually needed to accurately cut the bearings for the diamonds.

Fig. 4-9. Using a file to remove metal burrs that extend from the surface of the plate.

Fig. 4-10. Brush the bearing clear of debris before seating the diamond.

STEP 6 — SEAT THE DIAMONDS
(Fig. 4-9, 4-10, 4-11)

Figure 4-9 shows metal burrs, developed when the bearings were cut, being removed by filing to prepare the bearings for seating the diamonds. The filing should be done lightly to avoid removing the border engravings. Later twist the setting bur into each bearing briefly to further clean the bearing. Brush the remaining debris from the bearings and clean the diamonds.

Push the diamonds into the bearings. Some diamonds will go in easily while others might have to be pressured a little. Ideally the diamonds should require a certain amount of pressure to seat them snuggly. Despite the size variation it is preferable that the diamonds are all seated to a level where their tables are flush to the surface of the plate (assuming that all of the diamonds are small on the carat scale).

Fig. 4-11. Using a piece of wood to press the diamonds into the bearings.

Fig. 4-12. Shows a round graver being used to raise beads onto the diamonds.

STEP 7 — SECURE THE DIAMONDS
(Fig. 4-12)

Use a round graver to raise four beads onto each diamond. The trick is to raise the beads in line. This can be done by beginning each bead on the engraved lines the same distance from each diamond. In that manner the beads are less likely to be staggered. Do not try to tighten the diamonds until all the beads are partially raised, and the diamonds will remain level in the bearings. Too much pressure to raise one bead without the opposite bead securing the diamond from that side could cause the diamond to tilt.

STEP 8 — ENGRAVE EXCESS METAL

(Fig. 4-13)

The excess metal is engraved to expose the beads and diamonds. Use an onglette graver. First cut the metal at each corner down to the base of the bead there. These are short cuts but important in order to distinguish the square. They also help to keep the graver from slipping through the edge of the plate when the four side borders are carved. From then on all engravings should be beveled by slanting the graver. The four sides are carved from corner to corner along the bases of the beads and girdles of the diamonds to the edge of the plate.

The method of cutting up the metal between the beads is optional depending upon the intended design. The accompanying photographs show beveled rows of metal being bright cut between the diamonds. This is done by making long cuts across the plate as if to separate the diamonds into rows. Then the ring is turned to do the same in a cross cutting manner. The result is a slope of metal that rises to a ridge between each diamond.

Fig. 4-13. Shows an onglette graver being used to engrave excess metal between the diamonds.

Fig. 4-14. Shows a beading tool being used to shape the beads.

STEP 9 — SHAPE THE BEADS

(Fig. 4-14)

A beading tool is used to shape the beads. This is done before bright cutting to avoid damage to the bright cuts, and because some further removal of metal may be necessary to adequately form the beads. The beads should become perfectly rounded and equal in size. Flakes of metal often cling onto the diamonds from newly formed beads. These can be removed with a sharp flat graver.

STEP 10 — BRIGHT CUT THE METAL
(Fig. 4-15, 4-16, 4-17, 4-18)

The engraved metal is bright cut with a flat graver. The tip of the graver will have to be sharpened and polished often during the phase. First bright cut the metal between the diamonds because the graver tip is likely to ram into the borders. Then bright cut the four borders. Keep the graver slanted to assure a good beveled cut. Also use light shaving strokes until one lengthy stroke can be completed at each section. When completed, chase the corner cuts again with an onglette graver to the base of the corner beads. Finally use a flat hand file to trim the outside edge of the plate, then smooth it with a large rubber wheel. A milligrain can be applied after that.

Fig. 4-15. Using a flat graver to bright cut the metal.

Fig. 4-16. Trim the edge of the plate with a flat hand file.

Fig. 4-17. Using a large rubber wheel to smooth the edge of the plate.

Fig. 4-18. Applying a milligrain to the edge of the plate.

Fig. 4-19. Shows a square cluster of bead set diamonds.

2

Round Cluster

Round plates are traditionally used for pavé setting diamonds into clusters. An eminent feature is that they are almost always stamped into a dome. Their use is also universally accepted in all types of jewelry because several diamonds can be grouped together in them to resemble one large, brilliant cut diamond. This segment illustrates a specific configuration of diamonds that can be applied to obtain that effect. It is a seven diamond cluster with each diamond being equal in size.

Round clusters having either seven or nineteen diamonds of equal sizes are perfect examples of how multiple diamonds can be set to resemble a single larger diamond. When seven diamonds are applied, one is set in the center and six surround it. A nineteen diamond round cluster, being similar but an extended version, likewise has six diamonds surrounding a center but also has twelve diamonds encircling those. In both situations there is a unique uniformity in that all diamonds can be set girdle-to-girdle to form a cylindrical figure.

When a round cluster has unequal sizes of diamonds, or total number other than seven or nineteen, the diamonds might not be set quite so symmetrical. However, diamonds of varying sizes can also be joined to form a round cluster. There will always be a certain amount of planning involved when this occurs in order to arrange the diamonds in the best possible layout. This is an exercise where the diamond setter must perceive the result of the work before starting it.

Pavé setting diamonds into a round plate is a recurring task of the diamond setter. Perhaps the jewelry market has a greater demand for the round shape because it resembles a traditional round diamond. Manufacturers apply the fixed pattern of both the seven and nineteen diamonds because they are geometrically capable of covering the surface of a round plate. Customers, whose diamonds are usually mixed sizes, often select the alternative of having their diamonds set into a round cluster. In those situations the diamond setter is provided with the ultimate challenge of assembling diamonds in a manner that will conceal the metal. A diamond setter can set hundreds of round clusters and learn something new from each one.

STEP 1 — INSPECT THE MOUNTING

(Fig. 4-20)

Checklist:

(a) Use a millimeter gauge to measure the thickness of the plate. Be sure that the bearings can be cut low enough that the diamonds will seat properly without falling through. Dome shaped plates such as the one in figure 4-20 sometimes have too much metal removed when assembling to the mounting. All areas of the plate should be measured.

(b) The plate should be high enough that after the diamonds are set, their culets will not protrude into the finger space of the ring.

(c) A visual inspection of this mounting shows that the plate is well supported by the undergallery, but the ring shank is thin. A mental note should be taken in these situations to avoid bending the shank when pressure is applied to raise the beads later.

(d) Before any work is done to the mounting, be confident that all of the diamonds will fit into the plate.

Fig. 4-20. Shows a round cluster mounting.

Fig. 4-21. Adjust the dividers from three randomly spaced points on the edge of the plate to find the center point.

STEP 2 — DESIGN A LAYOUT

(Fig. 4-21, 4-22, 4-23, 4-24)

The series of photographs for this segment show seven equal size diamonds being set into a round plate. Six diamonds will eventually surround one in the center. The center point is found by trial-and-error using dividers. To do this adjust the dividers from three randomly spaced points on the outside edge of the plate until three arcs cross in the center (see fig. 4-21).

Next, find the radius of the six surrounding center points for those diamonds. This is done by placing the center diamond on the center point and another diamond adjacent to it anywhere just so there is a slight separation between them. (After the diamonds are seated, they will join closer.) Engrave a tick mark on each side of the second diamond to designate the proposed radius (see fig. 4-22). Remove the diamonds and engrave the radius circle from the center point of the plate through the tick marks (see fig. 4-23). This will be the center line of the six surrounding diamonds.

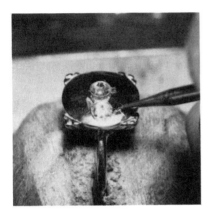

Fig. 4-22. Engrave tick marks alongside a second diamond to begin the center line of the surrounding diamonds.

Fig. 4-23. Using dividers to engrave the center line of the surrounding diamonds.

To find the center points of the six surrounding diamonds, first use a round graver to make a depression on the radius circle — preferably along the finger line of the ring. This beginning location is an option that will have the favorable result of a row of three diamonds on the finger line of the ring (see fig. 4-37). Now, using the same previous adjustment of the dividers used to engrave the radius circle, begin from the depression and swivel the dividers until the other point can cross an arc on the circle (see fig. 4-24). From that arc swivel the dividers again to engrave another arc farther along the circle. By continuing this pattern the divider point should eventually conclude at the original indentation leaving six equally spaced arcs on the circle. Those are the center points of the six surrounding diamonds.

Fig. 4-24. Using dividers to mark six equally spaced center points.

Fig. 4-25. Shows holes being drilled into a round plate.

STEP 3 — DRILL THE HOLES
(Fig. 4-25)

Use a round graver to pick a depression into the center point of the plate and the six surrounding center points. These will be starter holes for the drill to keep it from slipping. Drill the holes cautiously so that the drill is controlled when it completes a hole. The drill could break if it rams the undergallery.

STEP 4 — TAPER BORE THE HOLE
(Fig. 4-26)

The center hole is taper bored first to ensure that when the surrounding holes are being bored they can be kept from overlapping the center. Maintain a good taper from the surface of the plate by not permitting the bud bur to go too far into the metal. Also, do not cut a bore wider than the diameter of the diamonds. When pavé setting diamonds close together, such as in this case, it is often advisable to go ahead and cut the bearing for the center diamond. Then return to bore the holes for the surrounding diamonds.

Fig. 4-26. Using a bud bur to taper bore the holes.

Fig. 4-27. Shows the bearings being cut with a high speed setting bur.

STEP 5 — CUT THE BEARINGS
(Fig. 4-27)

A high speed setting bur is used to cut the bearings. There will undoubtedly be at least one diamond that is at least slightly larger than the others. That diamond should be set into the center if all of the diamonds are the same quality. A compromise of quality versus size is always a decision to be pondered when setting clusters.

STEP 6 — SEAT THE DIAMONDS
(Fig. 4-28)

Clean the bearings and diamonds before seating the diamonds. Particles between the bearings and diamonds could cause an improper seat and could be difficult to remove later. If a little pressure is necessary to push the diamonds into the bearings, try using a piece of wood placed against the table facets. The diamonds being set in the series of photographs are small on the carat scale. They are all set with their tables flush to the surface of the plate. Larger diamonds should be set slightly higher (see fig. 2-19, pg. 62).

Fig. 4-28. Seating the diamonds by pressing them into the bearing with a piece of wood.

STEP 7 — SECURE THE DIAMONDS
(Fig. 4-29A, 4-29B)

Raise the beads onto the center diamond first. In this manner the beads of the surrounding diamonds can symmetrically begin from the grooves left by the round graver. To raise the beads onto the center diamond, begin from a common distance between the surrounding diamonds. Raise the beads from opposite sides of the diamond a little at a time until the diamond can be secured without tilting out of level. Then raise the beads onto the surrounding diamonds. Those beads should begin from the grooves left by the round graver to secure the center diamond. The beads around the border of the plate should begin between the diamonds so that when completed the beads will not interfere with the circular bright cut that will be made later. See figure 4-29B to visualize the bead locations.

Fig. 4-29. (A) Raising beads onto the diamonds to secure them.

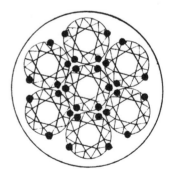

Fig. 4-29. (B) Shows placement of beads on a seven diamond-round cluster.

STEP 8 — ENGRAVE EXCESS METAL
(Fig. 4-30)

Using an onglette graver, first carve a bevel around the six surrounding diamonds from the girdles to the edge of the plate. The metal between the diamonds is then star cut. Do this by making straight beveled cuts from girdle level removing the metal along the side of each bead. The cuts in the center of the plate conclude between the trios of beads, and the cuts adjacent to the surrounding beads conclude at the base of the beveled border.

Fig. 4-30. Using an onglette graver to engrave excess metal.

Fig. 4-31. Shows a beading tool being used to "round off" the beads.

STEP 9 — SHAPE THE BEADS
(Fig. 4-31)

Be sure that the beads are exposed before attempting to shape them. If the metal around the beads is not sufficiently trimmed away, the beads will not form properly. Since the beads are very close together, especially near the center of the plate, the concave tip of the beading tool should be well shaped. Any excess metal at the tip of the beading tool should be ground away.

STEP 10 — BRIGHT CUT THE METAL
(Fig. 4-32, 4-33, 4-34, 4-35, 4-36)

The star engravings between the beads and diamonds are bright cut first. This is done with the polished tip of a flat graver simply by chasing over the short carvings that were made previously by the onglette graver. The circular border is bright cut last. That section is more tedious to bright cut because of the contour and its length. It will help to plane the metal as much as feasible before polishing the tip of the flat graver. (A polished tip will become dull quickly if it is subjected to so much cutting.) The recommendation is to first use short shaving strokes to plane the border. Then, after sharpening the tip again, polish it to make long continuous bright cuts. Remember that a flat graver must be held at a low angle to the plate to avoid chopping the metal.

The design of the ring in the series of photographs requires that the plate has had to be soldered onto four prongs. Now each of those prongs should be shaped to resemble having three beads. To do this first separate the beads by sawing a little on each side of the center bead to a common center point between the three at the edge of the plate. Do not saw too deep, but just enough that a cup bur can be used to round off the beads. Afterwards use a three corner needle file and a knife edge pumice wheel to remove the ridges that form on the beaded metal from the cup bur. The same file is then used to trim the edge of the plate. Applying a milligrain around the edge of the plate is optional.

Fig. 4-32. Using a flat graver to bright cut the metal.

Fig. 4-33. Shows a saw being used to separate the corner prongs just enough that a cup bur can be used to "round off" three beads at each corner.

Fig. 4-34. Shows a cup bur being used to "round off" three beads at each prong.

Fig. 4-35. Shows a three corner needle file being used to trim the edge of the plate between the prongs.

Fig. 4-36. Using a knife edge pumice wheel to smooth the edge of the plate.

Fig. 4-37. Shows seven diamonds bead set into a round cluster.

3

Oval Cluster

Objectives of pavé setting diamonds into oval plates are similar in many respects to that of round plates. The primary purpose of both designs is to display a cluster of diamonds in a configuration that will resemble one large diamond. In this case it is an oval cut diamond. However, there is an adequate quantity of unique procedural differences to warrant a segment specializing in pavé setting diamonds into oval shaped plates.

Uniform arrangements of diamonds are available when setting selected numbers of equal size diamonds into an oval plate. Unfortunately these numbers are not as consistant in an oval as they are in a round plate because the arcs of various ovals differ. For instance, one oval figure may accept ten equal size diamonds — two adjacent rows of three diamonds set across the width, and two diamonds at each end. Setting the same diamonds into another oval having the same surface area might not fill the plate. This is because two ovals having the same surface area may differ in length and width.

Often, like the round cluster, mixed numbers and sizes of diamonds must be set into an oval. At times carefully planned patterns of mixed diamonds offer a better arrangement to cover the metal. This is especially true in oval plates because of the figure itself. By referring to the layout phase of the bead setting procedure in SECTION II, the diamond setter might find that certain diamonds seem to belong in particular areas of the plate. Since an oval is a mass of tapers and curves, it may be more beneficial for pavé purposes to set mixed sizes of diamonds that can be selectively spaced.

The likes and differences of pavé setting round and oval clusters are somewhat contradictory. The purpose of each is clearly stated as the adornment of a larger diamond or blanket of diamonds. In regards to design, one may be selected over the other for preference of a particular shape. The diamond setter's business here is to decide which is the most advantageous layout. Given a selection of diamonds and a mounting, a schematic has to be devised to assemble them in accordance with the provisions of pavé setting. The pavé possibilities, concerning the variations of diamonds, depend equally upon the relation between the length and width of the oval figure.

The example to pavé set diamonds into an oval cluster illustrated in this

162

segment involves four different sizes of diamonds. There are eleven diamonds total to be grouped as a cluster. Situations such as this usually occur during a special order — remount job. Using this example emphasizes the layout phase of the bead setting procedure. Because of the unequal number and size of the diamonds, a plan is first devised to arrange the diamonds where they will obtain the maximum pavé effect. At the same time the diamonds as a group should also resemble an oval shape.

STEP 1 — INSPECT THE MOUNTING

(Fig. 4-38, 4-39)

Checklist:

(a) Check the thickness of the plate to see if the diamonds can be seated to an adequate depth without falling through. A millimeter degree gauge should be used to do this because the edge of the plate might be built up more than the center.

(b) Determine if the culets of the diamonds will extend into the finger space of the ring after the diamonds are set. This can be done visually by placing the largest diamond to the side of the plate and undergallery. Figure 4-39 shows the diamond being handled with bees wax and lowered to the approximate level where it will be after seating.

(c) Inspect the mounting for strength. Anticipate the effects of the pressure that will be projected to the plate, undergallery, and ring shank.

(d) Arrange the diamonds on the plate to be sure there is enough space for all of the diamonds to be set.

Fig. 4-38. Shows a ring with an oval cluster plate.

Fig. 4-39. Using bees wax to hold a diamond to the side of the plate.

STEP 2 — DESIGN A LAYOUT
(Fig. 4-40, 4-41, 4-42)

Various sizes of diamonds being set into an oval plate are shown in the photographs. To begin the layout process, the plate is first heated just enough to apply a thin film of bees wax on it (see fig. 4-40). The diamonds can then be placed on the plate without easily falling off. After the most advantageous arrangement is laid out on the plate, a scriber is used to engrave boundaries between and around the diamonds (see fig. 4-41)

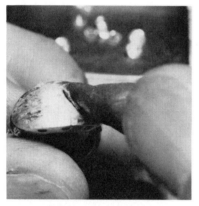

Fig. 4-40. Smearing bees wax on a warm mounting to lay out the diamonds.

Fig. 4-41. Using a scriber during the lay out to engrave boundaries between and around the diamonds.

After the boundary markings have been engraved, carve a sketch of the oval plate into the wax at the inside bottom of a tin pillbox (see fig. 4-42). Remove the diamonds from the plate one at a time and place them into their corresponding locations on the sketch. This is done for safe-keeping and for reference later as the bearings are cut to seat each diamond into a particular location.

Fig. 4-42. Diamonds layed out in a tin for referal to their proper location later as each diamond is set.

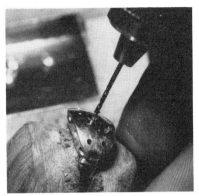

Fig. 4-43. Drilling holes into an oval cluster plate.

STEP 3 — DRILL THE HOLES
(Fig. 4-43)

Indent the center points where the diamonds are to be set. A round graver can be used to do this. The indentations will serve to keep the drill from slipping. The holes can then be drilled safely and accurately.

STEP 4 — TAPER BORE THE HOLES
(Fig. 4-44, 4-45)

Since various sizes of diamonds are to be set, the diameters of the bores should vary accordingly. This will require a certain amount of tool changing in order to use the appropriate bud bur for each bore. Figure 4-45 shows the oval plate after the holes are taper bored.

Fig. 4-44. Taper boring the holes with a bud bur.

Fig. 4-45. Shows the holes in an oval plate after being taper bored.

STEP 5 — CUT THE BEARINGS

(Fig. 4-46)

High speed setting burs are used to cut the bearings. If the diamonds will not be set too close together, cut the bearings for the smaller diamonds first regardless of their locations. Otherwise, start from the center of the plate and work toward the ends. The diamonds will have to be used to test each bearing as it is cut. The bearings are tested to avoid cutting the bearings too deep or too shallow.

Fig. 4-46. Shows a high speed setting bur being used to cut the bearings.

Fig. 4-47. Shows the burrs of metal that often extend from the holes under the plate.

STEP 6 — SEAT THE DIAMONDS

(Fig. 4-47, 4-48, 4-49)

First prepare the plate for seating the diamonds. The surface of the plate and the underside should be smooth. The surface can be filed, but the metal burrs extending from the underside are removed by a setting bur (see fig. 4-48). The bearings and diamonds are then cleaned, and the diamonds placed into their perspective bearings.

Fig. 4-48. Shows a setting bur being used to remove the burrs of metal under the plate.

Fig. 4-49. Shows a piece of wood being used to press the diamonds into the bearings.

STEP 7 — SECURE THE DIAMONDS

(Fig. 4-50A, 4-50B, 4-50C)

Use a round graver to raise the beads onto the diamonds. The oval plate in the photographs is engraved between the beads, but the metal could just as well be beaded between the diamonds. This decision has to be made at this time because it will determine the locations of the beads.

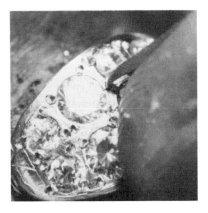

Fig. 4-50. (A) Shows a round graver being used to "raise the beads" to secure the diamonds.

If the metal is to be engraved later, as in this case, the beads are raised symmetrically around and between the diamonds. Where a bead is raised to secure a diamond, there must be another bead across from it to secure an adjacent diamond. This is done in order to uniformly engrave the excess metal later. (Study the placement of the beads in figure 4-50B.) On the other hand, if the beaded design is elected, as shown in figure 4-50C, then the beads that secure the diamonds are randomly spaced.

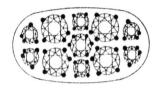

Fig. 4-50. (B) Shows the placement of beads if the excess metal is to be engraved.

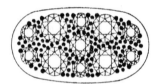

Fig. 4-50. (C) Shows the placement of beads if the excess metal is to be beaded.

STEP 8 — ENGRAVE EXCESS METAL

(Fig. 4-51)

Use an onglette graver to engrave the metal. The border should be engraved first. Remove the metal a little at a time from the girdles of the diamonds to the edge of the plate. Begin by making short straight cuts from alongside the girdle of one diamond passing by the bases of the beads to the girdle of an adjacent diamond. Eventually larger cuts can be made until the entire border is beveled around the diamonds.

The metal between the diamonds is engraved next to expose the beads and diamonds. The simplest manner of doing this is as follows: carve the metal away from the sides of each bead beginning from the girdle of the diamond that bead secures; carve straight to the base of the adjacent bead that secures an adjacent diamond; all cuts should be beveled away from the beads and girdles of the diamonds.

Fig. 4-51. Shows an onglette graver being used to engrave the metal between the diamonds.

Fig. 4-52. Using a beading tool to shape the beads.

STEP 9 — SHAPE THE BEADS

(Fig. 4-52)

The beads will vary in size. This is because of the amount of metal that was available at each location to raise a bead, and also because larger beads may have been desired on larger diamonds. Such is the case shown in the photographs of the oval cluster. For those reasons the beading tools used to shape the beads will be different depending on the sizes of the beads.

STEP 10 — BRIGHT CUT THE METAL

(Fig. 4-53, 4-54, 4-55, 4-56)

Use a flat graver having a polished tip to bright cut the metal. First bright cut the metal between the diamonds, then the border. One particularly frustrating area to bright cut on some oval plates is the short curved ends. This is a common problem on any short curve. To compensate, an alternative means of bright cutting may be selected (see Alternative Means of Bright Cutting, pg. 85).

If the metal at the short curves is choppy after bright cutting, revert to an alternative means to supplement it. To perfect the bright cut, the metal can be burnished with a $\frac{3}{32}$ inch shaft that has a polished tip at the tapered end (see fig. 4-54). Later a barrette needle file can be used to trim the outside edge of the plate. A milligrain applied around the edge of the plate is optional.

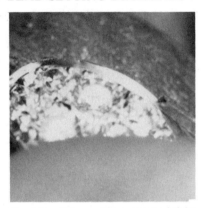

Fig. 4-53. Using a flat graver to bright cut the metal.

Fig. 4-54. Using a tapered ³⁄₃₂ inch bur shaft, that has been polished at the tip, to burnish the curve of metal until it becomes bright.

Fig. 4-55. Using a barrette needle file to trim the edge of the plate.

Fig. 4-56. Shows the edge of the plate being milligrained.

Fig. 4-57. A oval shaped cluster of bead set diamonds.

Pear Cluster

To advance the illustrations of pavé setting clusters, a pear shape is introduced at this time. Being a traditional diamond cut figure, it is also a popular request. Setting diamonds into a pear shape plate is a little more involved than the previous clusters because the metal tapers to a point. If no smaller diamonds are furnished that will cover the area sufficiently, the pavé effects could be hampered. Problem solving in this case will require skillful engraving techniques to adequately replicate those missing facets. This segment will illustrate the necessary steps to overcome that deficiency and other implications of pavé setting a pear shape cluster.

STEP 1 — INSPECT THE MOUNTING
(Fig. 4-58)

Checklist:

(a) Use a millimeter degree gauge to measure the thickness of the plate. Be certain that the bearings can be cut to an adequate depth in order to seat the diamonds properly.

(b) Check to see that the plate is high enough. After the diamonds are set, the culets should not protrude into the finger area.

(c) Inspect the mounting for strength. A brief visual inspection is all that is usually necessary, but some mountings such as the one in figure 4-58 could be deceptive. Wide spans of metal should be measured for thickness by a millimeter degree gauge. If it is very thin, care will have to be taken during the diamond setting procedure to avoid collapsing it.

(d) The final inspection is done to see that there is plenty of space on the plate for the diamonds to be set.

STEP 2 — DESIGN A LAYOUT
(Fig. 4-59)

Lay out the diamonds tables down on the plate. The smallest diamond should be set at the point and the largest in the center. All diamonds surrounding the center should be equally spaced from each other. Then engrave boundaries between and around the girdles of the diamonds. The border between the girdles of the diamonds and the edge of the plate is engraved by dividers after the diamonds are removed. Lastly, the centers where each diamond will be set are marked between the boundaries that were made between and around the diamonds.

Fig. 4-58. A ring with a pear shaped cluster plate.

Fig. 4-59. Using a scriber to engrave border markings between and around the diamonds during the layout.

STEP 3 — DRILL THE HOLES

(Fig. 4-60)

Use a round graver to indent the plate metal at each center point, then drill the holes. Continually submerge the tip of the drill into a coolant to reduce friction between the drill and the metal. This will help the drill to cut into the metal and preserve the sharpness of the cutting lips on the drill.

Fig. 4-60. Drilling holes into a pear shaped cluster plate.

Fig. 4-61. Taper boring the holes with a bud bur.

STEP 4 — TAPER BORE THE HOLES

(Fig. 4-61)

Use a bud bur to taper bore the holes. First bore the center hole so that the space for setting the center diamond will be reserved. Then taper bore the surrounding holes. Remove a little metal at a time from all of the surrounding holes in case any of the bores will need to be adjusted for equal spacing.

STEP 5 — CUT THE BEARINGS

(Fig. 4-62)

Following the sequence of the previous step, cut the bearing for the center diamond first. Use high speed setting burs. Afterwards cut the bearings for the surrounding diamonds. Remember that various sizes of diamonds will be located in specific areas. Those diamonds will have to be separated and their locations marked.

Fig. 4-62. Cutting the bearings with a high speed setting bur.

STEP 6 — SEAT THE DIAMONDS

(Fig. 4-63, 4-64, 4-65, 4-66)

A preliminary step to seating the diamonds is to first clean the bearings and diamonds. This is done to ensure that there is no interference between them. File the metal protrusions (burrs) that extend above the plate from the newly cut bearings. Then re-insert a setting bur into each bearing and twist it briefly to remove clinging metal. Next, brush the remaining debris from the bearings. Finally remove bees wax and other materials from the diamonds (see Clean the Diamond, pg. 67).

Fig. 4-63. Using a barrette needle file to remove metal burrs that extend from the bearings.

Fig. 4-64. Brushing the bearings to remove loose debris.

After the preliminaries are completed, the diamonds are seated into their perspective bearings. Figure 4-65 shows the diamonds being handled by bees wax to place them into the bearings. Only the table facets of the diamonds are touched. When pushing the diamonds into the bearings, a little pressure is favorable. This will signify a good seat. A piece of wood could be used to push the diamonds into the bearings, but a soft metal rod such as brass, copper, or silver is acceptable. If the diamonds do not fit tight, a fingernail can be used to seat the diamonds.

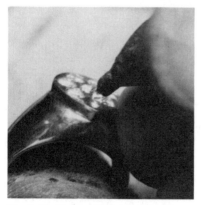

Fig. 4-65. Shows diamonds being handled by bees wax to place them into the bearings.

Fig. 4-66. Using a piece of wood to press the diamonds into the bearings.

STEP 7 — SECURE THE DIAMONDS

(Fig. 4-67)

Beginning with the center diamond, use a round graver to raise the beads onto the diamonds. First pry burrs of metal up to and slightly over all the diamonds. After being assured that the diamonds will remain level, the beads can be raised up and onto the diamonds to secure them. This is done by tilting the round graver to a higher angle while pushing the tip to the plate.

Fig. 4-67. Using a round graver to "raise the beads" to secure the diamonds.

Fig. 4-68. Shows an onglette graver being used to remove the excess metal before bright cutting.

STEP 8 — ENGRAVE EXCESS METAL

(Fig. 4-68)

Engrave or remove all of the metal between the diamonds and beads. The border metal that outlines the pear shape is cut first. Begin by making a short cut from the point of the pear to the base of the bead there. To bevel the border metal from the girdles of the diamonds and beads to the edge of the plate, hold the onglette graver at a slant. The border metal should be carved to the point of the pear from both sides. After the border metal is beveled, the metal between the diamonds is engraved.

In some areas between the diamonds a star cut might be warranted. Other areas might require nothing more than a thin straight cut to remove metal. To make the star cuts, the metal adjacent to each bead is carved at a bevel from the girdle of the diamond that it secures. Continue carving the metal in a straight path to the base of the nearest bead that secures an adjacent diamond. Repeat the cuts wherever possible.

STEP 9 — SHAPE THE BEADS

(Fig. 4-69)

Use a beading tool that has a suitable concave tip to round off the beads. The beading tool may be inserted into a wood handle to be used by hand, or it can be used in the handpiece of a flex-shaft machine (see Shape The Beads, pg. 77).

Fig. 4-69. Shows a beading tool being used to "round off the beads".

STEP 10 — BRIGHT CUT THE METAL

(Fig. 4-70, 4-71, 4-72)

The metal between the diamonds is bright cut first. This will require short shaving strokes with a flat graver. The graver will have to be sharpened and its tip polished after every few cuts. After the metal between the diamonds is brightened, the border is bright cut. This should be done with long shaving strokes that plane the metal. Short, choppy strokes might have to be applied first to remove high spots. Once the metal is reasonably smooth, the longer extended bright cuts are made. The final cuts on each side of the border are made into the point of the pear (see fig. 4-70).

Trim the edge of the plate with a barrette needle file. This is done to perfect the contour of the pear shape. The edge is beveled by the file to the crest of the bright cut. Afterwards emery the filed metal, then smooth it further with a large rubber wheel. Finally, a line of decorative beads to enhance the design can be engraved around the edge of the plate with a milligrain tool.

Fig. 4-70. Using a flat graver to bright cut the metal.

Fig. 4-71. Using a barrette needle file to trim the edge of the plate.

Fig. 4-72. Shows the edge of the plate being milligrained.

Fig. 4-73. Shows a cluster of diamonds bead set into a pear shaped plate.

5

Freestyle Cluster

The final segment of this section is a series of illustrations to pavé set several diamonds into a cluster. It is a classic example of pavé setting. The distinguishing feature is that there is no consistant border to control the diamonds. Upon completion the diamonds should coat the surface as they extend down the sides of the mounting. In accordance with pavé setting, the diamonds should also be set girdle-to-girdle with each conforming to the slope of the metal at its location. In this manner the perspective plane across their tables will follow the contour of the mounting.

STEP 1 — INSPECT THE MOUNTING
(Fig. 4-74)

Checklist:

(a) Measure the thickness of the metal. Use a millimeter degree gauge to measure all areas of the plate to be sure that all of the bearings can be cut to the proper depth.

(b) Determine if all of the diamonds can be set without having any of the culets extend to the finger of the wearer.

(c) Visually check the structure of the ring for strength in order to foresee any problems that might occur when pressure is applied to it.

(d) Check to see that there is enough space on the ring for all of the diamonds to be set.

STEP 2 — DESIGN A LAYOUT
(Fig. 4-75, 4-76, 4-77)

Thirty-seven diamonds are shown in the photographs being pavé set into a dome. In order to lay the diamonds out for spacing, a film of bees wax is spread on the setting areas. Figure 4-75 shows the mounting being heated by a flame. The mounting need only become warm enough for the bees wax to melt when it is applied. Then the diamonds can be shifted about without easily falling off of the ring. Figure 4-76 shows the diamonds table down on the metal. A flat graver is used to press on the culets of the diamonds to secure them into the bees wax. The flat graver is used in this particular situation because it is not bulky. Precise adjustments can be made, and it is less likely to slip.

Fig. 4-74. Shows a pavé cluster mounting.

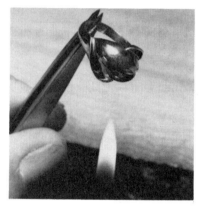

Fig. 4-75. Shows a mounting being warmed by a small flame in order to smear bees wax onto it during the layout phase.

After the spacing is completed to the best advantage, the diamonds are removed one at a time. The diamonds shown in the photographs being set are assumed to be approximately the same size. However, because of slight variations of size or quality, the locations of some diamonds may be specific. Those diamonds should be segregated and their locations marked. As each diamond is removed (using a round graver) the center point is estimated and marked by sticking the tip of the round graver into the metal (see fig. 4-77). Only a noticeable mark is made at this time. To avoid having the graver slip and jerk other diamonds off of the metal, the center points are indented for drilling purposes later.

Fig. 4-76. Using a flat graver to press the diamonds to the bees wax for better adherence during the layout phase.

Fig. 4-77. Using a round graver to mark the center point of each diamond as they are removed.

STEP 3 — DRILL THE HOLES
(Fig. 4-78)

During this stage the center points are farther indented by the round graver, and the holes are drilled. The indentations should keep the drill from slipping off center. Drill all holes perpendicular to the metal.

Fig. 4-78. Drilling holes into a pavé cluster mounting.

Fig. 4-79. Using a bud bur to taper bore the holes.

STEP 4 — TAPER BORE THE HOLES

(Fig. 4-79)

All the holes are taper bored at least partially before cutting any bearings. Continually check the spacing of bores to be sure that none begin to overlap. Adjustments can be made at this time by tilting the bud bur to "pull the holes."

STEP 5 — CUT THE BEARINGS

(Fig. 4-80)

High speed setting burs are used to cut the bearings. Although a large number of diamonds are said to be the same size, that is seldom true in reality. In order to perfectly seat the diamonds later, some bearings will have to be cut slightly smaller or larger to accommodate certain diamonds (see Cut The Bearing, pg. 60).

Fig. 4-80. Shows a high speed setting bur being used to cut the bearings.

Fig. 4-81. Shows a barrette needle file being used to remove metal burrs that extend from the bearings.

STEP 6 — SEAT THE DIAMONDS

(Fig. 4-81, 4-82, 4-83, 4-84)

File the metal burrs down that rise from the crest of the bearings. These are commonly developed when the bearings are cut. If the burrs are not removed, the actual depth of the bearings could be perceived as being deeper than they actually are. Also use a setting bur or hart bur to remove metal burrs that form at the opening of the holes underneath the plate (see fig. 4-82 & 4-83). After the bearings and diamonds are cleaned, the diamonds can be seated.

Fig. 4-82. Shows metal burrs that develop from the holes under the plate.

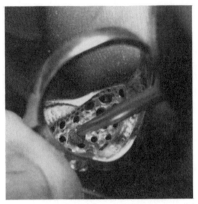

Fig. 4-83. Using a hart bur to remove metal burrs under the plate.

Begin seating the diamonds into the center bearing and work toward the extremities. By seating the diamonds in this sequence, overlapping can be prevented and the finer quality diamonds can be assured of being set into the center. When several diamonds are being set, groups of diamonds should be secured by going ahead and raising the beads (see Step 7 of this segment.) This will help to maintain control over the work.

Fig. 4-84. Seating the diamonds by pressing them into the bearings.

Fig. 4-85. Using a round graver to secure a group of diamonds before seating all of them.

STEP 7 — SECURE THE DIAMONDS

(Fig. 4-85)

When pavé setting a compact cluster of diamonds, there is usually very little metal remaining between the diamonds. What metal does exist will have to be used to secure the diamonds, thus causing the beads to be randomly spaced. Also, since multiple beads will be raised from a small space of metal between a group of diamonds, that metal will have to be used sparingly. In effect, when using the round graver, the basic method of raising a bead might have to be shortened. Some beads will be raised by pushing the tip of the round graver straight down into the metal rather than beginning from a distance at a lower angle (see Section II - Secure The Diamond, pg. 70).

STEP 8 — ENGRAVE EXCESS METAL
(Fig. 4-86)

The excess metal in this case is, for the most part, around the edge of the cluster. The metal that remains between the diamonds is beaded even though many of the beads do not actually secure any diamonds. The manner in which the metal at the edge of the cluster is engraved might be inconsistant. For example, figure 4-86 shows that there are some sections that require an onglette graver to remove a path of metal alongside the diamonds. That section is later bright cut. On the other hand, figure 4-89 shows a section of the plate where there is no border. The metal there is simply cut from the girdles of the diamonds, past the beads, and through the edge of the plate.

Fig. 4-86. Use an onglette graver to remove excess metal wherever possible.

STEP 9 — SHAPE THE BEADS

(Fig. 4-87, 4-88)

Rounding off the beads in some designs such as the one presented here is often cumbersome. A beading tool is commonly used but requires periodic re-shaping to refine the concave tip. A simplified version shown in figure 4-88 demonstrates the use of a round graver to round off the beads. This is done by lightly scraping the beads in all directions (see Shape The Beads, pg. 79).

Fig. 4-87. Shows a beading tool being used to shape the beads.

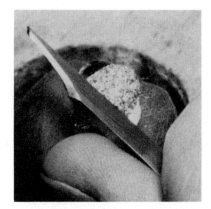

Fig. 4-88. Shows the option of using a round graver to shape the beads.

STEP 10 — BRIGHT CUT THE METAL

(Fig. 4-89, 4-90, 4-91)

Bright cut the metal that was previously engraved by the onglette graver. One particular area of concern is the border shown in figure 4-86. A smaller size flat graver, such as a No. 39, might have to be used in those situations in order to avoid cutting into metal that is not intended to be engraved. Other metal as shown in figure 4-89 is bright cut through the edge of the plate to flash the metal. When the bright cutting is completed, the areas of the mounting that were distorted or scratched during the procedure are refinished. This is done with the use of files, emery paper, and rubber wheels.

Fig. 4-89. Shows a flat graver being used to bright cut the metal through the edge of the plate to flash the metal.

Fig. 4-90. Using a barrette needle file to remove scratches from the mounting.

Fig. 4-91. Using a knife edge pumice wheel to smooth the outlining areas of the mounting.

Fig. 4-92. Shows a bead set pavé cluster.

AFTERWORD

Bead setting diamonds into a pavé cluster is an appropriate conclusion to *BEAD SETTING DIAMONDS With Pavé Applications.* The organization of the book is designed to gradually progress from simplicity to more complex. Hopefully the reader has not misinterpreted any descriptive material, nor skimmed any familiar presentations that may have been included as a lead to an informative notation. Although each segment follows a basic procedure there are unlimited adaptations and strategies of completion. Given that there are alternate means of accomplishing the applications presented in this book there can really never be an ending per se. Whatever degree of communication has been established it is the author's intention that skills to bead set diamonds will either develop or begin from here.

SUGGESTED READINGS

Bauer, Max, *Precious Stones*, Vol. 1, Trans. L. J. Spencer (1904; rpt. New York; Dover Publications, Inc. 1968)
   Contains authoritative information on diamonds.

Budinski, Kenneth G., *Engineering Materials: Properties And Selection* (Reston, Virginia: Reston Publishing Co. Inc., 1979).
   This book has very good sections covering the chemistry of metals.

Feirer, John L. and Lindbeck, John R., *Metalwork*, 2nd ed., (Peoria, Illinois: Chas. A. Bennett Co., Inc. 1970).
   Thorough metalworking book that teaches how to design, plan, and carry out a project.

Gregorietti, Guido, *Jewelry: History And Technique From Egyptians To The Present*, Trans. (New Jersey: Charlweil Books Inc., 1979).
   History and photographs of jewlery from each developmental era of jewelry making to the present.

Hardy, Allen R. and Bowman, John J., *The Engravers Manual* (New York: Van Nostrand-Reinhold Co., 1976).
   An excellent reference source for graver preparation and use.

Hemard, Larry, *Creative Jewelry Making* (Garden City, New York: Doubleday & Co. Inc., 1975).
   Fine photography of actual bead setting. Includes sections with line drawings of channel setting baguettes, star setting, and gypsy setting.

Jarvis, Charles A., *Jewelry Manufacture and Repair* (New York: Bonanza Books, 1979).
   Good sections on preparing plates and settings for diamond setting; includes drilling and laying out diamonds. Also a section on eternity rings.

McCreight, Tim, *Metalworking For Jewelry: Tools, Materials, Techniques* New York: Van Nostrand-Reinhold Co., 1979).
   Among other valuable information applicable to diamond setting this book describes in detail the techniques of moving metal.

Wooding, Robert R., *DIAMOND SETTING: The Professional Approach* (Erlanger, Kentucky: Dry Ridge Co., 1984).
   This book was written to teach diamond setting. It is basic enough to be understood by an apprentice, yet sufficiently in depth to benefit an experienced diamond setter.

DIAMOND SETTING SCHOOLS

BOWMAN TECHNICAL
SCHOOL
220 West King Street
Lancaster, PA. 17603

DRY RIDGE DIAMOND
SETTING SCHOOL
P.O. Box 18814
Erlanger, Kentucky
606/727-6650

GEM CITY COLLEGE
7th & State Street
Quincy, IL. 62301
217/222-0391

GEORGE BROWN COLLEGE
OF APPLIED ARTS & TECH.
Box 1015 Station B
Toronto, Canada M5T 2T9

GEMOLOGICAL INSTITUTE
OF AMERICA
P.O. Box 2110
Santa Monica, CA. 90406

HOLLAND SCHOOL
FOR JEWELERS
231 Broad Box 882
Selma, AL. 36701
205/872-3421

INSTITUTE OF
JEWELRY TRAINING
3901 Norwood Avenue-Suite B
Sacramento, CA. 95838

JEWELERS INSTITUTE
OF AMERICA
P.O. Box 66
Statesboro, Georgia 30458

THE JEWELRY INSTITUTE
40 Sims Avenue
Providence, R.I. 02909

MOHAVE COMMUNITY
COLLEGE
1977 W. Acoma Blvd.
Lake Havasu City, AZ. 86403

RAY SCHOW'S SCHOOL OF
DIAMOND SETTING
1826 N.E. 122nd
Portland, Oregon 97230
503/255-1116

REVERE ACADEMY OF
JEWELRY ARTS
760 Market Street-Suite 939
San Francisco, CA. 94102
415/391-4179

STEWARTS INTERNATIONAL
SCHOOL FOR JEWELERS
651 Indiantown Road
Jupiter, Florida 33458
305/746-7586

TRENTON JEWELRY
SCHOOLS
2505 Popular Avenue
Memphis, TN. 38112
TN. 1-800-582-9181
Others 1-800-238-9226

INDEX

INDEX (cont.)